Organisational change and the management of expertise

Organisational Behaviour and Management Series
Edited by Robert Goffee

An understanding of organisational behaviour has become an increasingly important component of modern management education and development. This new series addresses key issues in contemporary organisational studies. It includes rigorous theoretical and empirical analyses of work, organisations and their management from a variety of perspectives. Contributions from well established fields of study – for example, individual change and motivation group processes, theories of organisation and change – are represented as well as those which explore *new* areas – technological change and innovation, corporate culture, strategy and competitiveness, public sector management, gender relations, stress management and career development. Series authors are lecturers and researchers in organisational behaviour and related disciplines: sociology, anthropology, social psychology and industrial relations. All books in the series will be of interest to the practitioner and students on graduate, undergraduate and post-experience courses.

Already published

Management in Developing Countries
Edited by Alfred M. Jaeger and Rabindra N. Kanungo

The Biases of Management
Barbara Wake Carroll

Managing Through Organisation: The Management Process, Forms of Organisation and the Work of Managers
Colin Hales

Organisational change and the management of expertise

Janette Webb and David Cleary

London and New York

First published 1994
by Routledge
11 New Fetter Lane, London EC4P 4EE

Simultaneously published in the USA and Canada by Routledge
29 West 35th Street, New York, NY 10001

Typeset in Times by
NWL Editorial Services, Langport, Somerset TA10 9DG

Printed and bound in Great Britain by
Biddles Ltd, Guildford and King's Lynn

British Library Cataloguing in Publication Data
A catalogue record for this book is available from the British
Library.

Library of Congress Cataloging in Publication Data
A catalogue record for this book has been applied for.

ISBN 0–415–09189–6 (hbk)

Contents

Figures

Acknowledgements

We would like to thank all of the managers and engineers whose accounts of their work form the substance of this book. We are also grateful to colleagues participating in the Economic and Social Research Council (ESRC)/ Department of Trade and Industry (DTI) New Technologies and the Firm Initiative, who provided a sympathetic audience for early drafts of much of our material. We are indebted to the ESRC and the DTI for financial support. Edinburgh University Faculty of Social Science provided a small grant which initiated the study, and sabbatical leave for writing the book. The Department of Business Studies provided time and space for ethnographic work and the Research Centre for Social Sciences provided a support network and a meeting place for the exchange of ideas. Jean Milne was an efficient project secretary and Ann Cameron, Department of Business Studies, helped with production of the manuscript. Full-time and part-time MBA students at Edinburgh have provided an interested audience for some of the material and were instrumental in gaining access to some of our informants.

Thank you to Rob Goffee, at the London Business School, for his encouragement and his input into the book proposal, and to Rosemary Nixon and others at Routledge for co-ordinating the editorial work.

Personally, I (Janette) am indebted to Colin for his unswerving confidence in my ability to carry on research and writing through two pregnancies, the birth of our two daughters and the exhaustion of early motherhood! I also wish to thank him for his continuing practical support at home, despite the increasing demands made by his job. Lastly, Islay and Catherine have made me keep the need for academic achievement in perspective.

1   Introducing the issues

Some organisations are turning themselves nearly inside out, buying
formerly internal services from outside suppliers, forming strategic
alliances and supplier–customer partnerships that bring external relationships inside.

(Rosabeth Moss Kanter, *Harvard Business Review*, 1989, p. 85)

companies should now be defining their business interests in terms of
what they do for their customers. Knowledge of customers' needs should
determine strategy and the kinds of businesses that could deliver the
strategy. It is too costly to think otherwise.

(Peter Wilson, *Financial Times*, 5 December 1991)

Anyone looking at the business world today, like anyone looking at political
and economic change in the modern world in general, could be forgiven for
thinking of the ancient Chinese curse, 'May you live in interesting times'.
Interesting times, indeed. The way people do business, and in particular the
way managers manage and organisations organise themselves, has changed
out of all recognition in the last twenty years – or so you might believe,
judging by the number of new management textbooks and the evangelical
zeal with which managers quote proverbs and quips from the latest
management guru. There is, to an unusual degree, consensus amongst representatives of business, research establishments and policy bodies that the
structure of product markets and competition, and hence the framework of
economic activity, are undergoing radical and continuing transformations. In
the face of declining profitability in established industries, senior managers
are being exhorted to change the way they do business. Every accepted code
of conduct and planning device is up for question. Managers are not only
charged with the need to rejuvenate their own business, however; they are
also increasingly seen as able to provide solutions to relative economic
decline in Europe and North America. Where this new breed of

manager-heroes are most in evidence is, of course, Eastern Europe and the ex-Soviet Union: the shock troops of economic reform are the Western managers, bankers and consultants descending on factories and companies from Stettin to Vladivostock, where the new ethos of managing the market seems not so much a way of doing business as the means of transforming the basis of society.

There is no shortage of willing advisers in the business schools, management consultancies and government agencies. Although there is a plethora of material, ranging from airport tomes to academic articles, there is agreement, to an unusual degree, about both the nature of the problems and their solution. The problems, literally, are in the past. In the past organisations had traditional ways of doing things. In the past, organisations were hierarchies and everyone knew their place. In the past, product markets were more stable and the pace of innovation slower. In the past, economic performance was often disappointing, managers inward looking, conservative and risk avoiding. The solutions are, literally, in the present. Change and instability, far from being the enemy, is the key to success. Managers at all levels are expected to become more outward-looking, visionary, willing to take risks and to make mistakes. The tools of long-term planning are seen as cumbersome and inflexible. Instead, managers are exhorted to live in the present, and to delight in constant change and uncertainty. Managers are meant to change their ways from being planners who 'do things right' to becoming enterprising heroes who enthusiastically embrace the need to question whether they are doing the right things.

The framework for such a 'bias towards action' (Peters, 1987) is provided by a simpler organisational structure, vertical dis-integration (and reintegration through strategic partnerships) and the replacement of bureaucratic hierarchies with flexible networks. This means replacing functional boundaries with fluid project teams and specialists with hybrid all-rounders, able to see beyond the confines of their own niche. More or less explicit in much of this writing is the concern with the creation of a culture, or ethos, in the company which encourages teamwork, openness and commitment to senior management goals, while discouraging 'them and us' politicking and status-conscious patterns of interaction. Only through creating the right corporate culture, it is argued, can managers cultivate the essential skills and expertise amongst the workforce for continuous innovation. The success of the company is seen as dependent, not on the application of business plans, quantitative techniques and rigid formulae, but on the cultivation of people.

Expertise, however, is elusive and fuzzily defined, concerned with relationships rather than the supposedly hard facts of products and markets. Despite this, or, more probably, because of it, the notion of expertise at present serves as common currency between the academic and business communities: academics discuss it at conferences, they write about it in learned journals, they argue about its meaning, while managers agitate about getting it, deploying it, selling it, developing it, controlling it and using it to 'add value' and gain 'competitive edge'. In a prominent *Harvard Business Review* article on business strategy, Prahalad and Hamel (1990) argue that the cultivation of expertise (or, in their terminology, 'core competence') is vital to the future competitiveness of any business: 'in the long run competitiveness derives from an ability to build at lower cost and more speedily than competitors the core competences that spawn unanticipated products' (p. 81). The role of senior and corporate management is no longer about financial investment in new technology and processes, but should be to create the project teams whose intellectual capital produces competitive advantage (Jaikumar, 1986). Ultimately, this calls for radical change in the principles of management, away from an administrative focus on the detail of a specific niche, or on the capital budgeting process, towards a grand vision consolidating corporate wide technologies and skills into 'competences that empower individual businesses to adapt quickly to changing opportunities'(Prahalad and Hamel, 1990, p. 81). The absence of such a concern with expertise, they argue, will lead to the demise of the company.

In parallel with management concern with the development of new forms of in-house expertise, and the questioning of existing functional barriers, is the assertion that barriers between firms can be made more permeable. The idealised version of this is given by Peters (1991): 'we are moving from a "pre-Copernican" business world, where the individual company is at the centre of the universe, to a far more fluid "post-Copernican" environment, where each company is but one point in an extended network of equals' (p. 98). Boundaries between specialisms or between managers and managed or between organisations are meant to be dissolved, so that the only driving force is between a group and its customer (internal or external). The focus for such an organisation is the network of customer–supplier relationships. Partly derived from the current interest in total quality management (TQM), which advocates the need for every member of the workforce to be responsive to customers, internally and externally, and partly from a concern that Western business is over-obsessed with internal arrangements, links with customers are seen as the key to new insights on products and processes. Conversely the active management of suppliers is seen as an important means by which product quality can be improved and costs, incurred through inspection of goods, rework and delay, can be reduced.

Researchers have pointed out that informal inter-firm networks and proactive management of the supply chain may also provide significant sources of shared expertise. Clark and Staunton (1990) set out a prospectus for an approach to innovation studies which sees innovation as embodied in the combining of technology, social organisation and knowledge. This would mean moving beyond the firm as the unit of analysis to examine relationships between suppliers and users of technologies. It would allow us to explore the role of users in shaping innovations (Fleck, 1988) and to analyse the ability (or inability) of expert groups in one firm to identify, and integrate, external sources of expertise relevant to their business. The implication is that managers at all levels must become less inward looking and more concerned with external relationships (Morgan, 1988).

The network or organic organisation is seen as crucially dependent on reliable information which provides rapid feedback on internal, and external suppliers', performance and enables a responsive service to customers. Computer systems provide the medium for the information network and become the essential underpinning of an otherwise seamless web of business relationships. It is not just a question of information flows, however. The significant context for this debate is the rapid commercialisation of inform-ation and communication technologies (ICTs), which are seen as having the potential to reverse the conventional business equation between increasing range and quality of goods and increasing price. ICTs have a direct impact on productivity, efficiency and unit labour costs. Moreover they make the traditional distinction between 'hard' equipment-based notions of innovation and 'soft' process innovations difficult to maintain, particularly when they are used to co-ordinate and integrate activities. For many firms, the initial phase of computerisation was mainly concerned with cost reduction, through rationalisation of labour and job cuts. The current phase, however, is characterised by the attempt to use ICTs as a strategic management tool for the provision of flexible information systems (e.g. Zuboff, 1988; Friedman and Cornford, 1989; Dyerson and Roper, 1991).

There is as yet little elaborated knowledge of how to manage the implied organisational transitions, but there is increasing awareness that the cultivation of expertise is one of the keys to success. Effective development and integration of computer systems depends on the ability of management to create workable project teams, to overcome existing functional barriers to co-operation and to assimilate technical specialist and end user knowledge (Clark and Staunton,1990; Fleck, Webster and Williams, 1990). Internal and external ICT experts are influential because of their perceived ability to design, develop and run the systems and therefore to provide the desired competitive edge. Without these skilled specialists, and without the organisation structures to exploit and renew their knowledge, the perception is that the business will stagnate or fail. The power of such expert groups, however, also threatens established status relations, including those between competing management specialisms. In some cases ICTs are themselves treated as a means to break down barriers (Morgan, 1988) and to reverse management's progressive control over knowledge and information about the business (Zuboff, 1988). The attempted integration of computer systems across the business begins to put all conventional 'expertises' up for question. The stakes in the organisational relationship between managers and experts could hardly be higher, since what is at issue is the power to determine the status, salary and promotion prospects of individuals and occupational groups. Managers may want to abrogate to themselves the definition of who the experts are and what kinds of expertise are to be most valued and rewarded. This, however, is an extremely problematic enterprise because the organisation does not exist in an economic and social vacuum. Managers may not like it, but the fact is that companies are part of a wider society which has its own ideas and definitions about who experts are, what they do and how they should be treated.

The apparent 'common sense' of many of the above prescriptions is one of the reasons underlying the appeal of this new perspective on management and organisations. But that is mainly because words are cheap and easy; action is neither. Managers could be forgiven for raising a weary eyebrow and pointing out that performing such radical organisational surgery is never easy, and many will succumb, so to speak, while on the operating table, from post-trauma shock or paralysis. The reward for those who survive, however, is proportionately greater: the renaissance of the organisation and increased profitability.

There is a further complication with many of the prescriptions for change: it is hard to distinguish between what is being practised, with what results, inside businesses and what is purely rhetorical – so much hot air. In reality it might be argued that the language of strategic partnerships in a supply chain of equals disguises the fact that in major industrial sectors we are increasingly faced not with equals in free competition but with a few large organisations, dominant in each market, struggling over the terms and conditions of exchange and looking for yet greater degrees of control through alliances and associations. How this translates into changes at the organisational level is unknown. In empirical surveys and case studies there is deep disagreement over what we are witnessing and whether it constitutes real change (Morris and Wood, 1991). Commenting on responses to a worldwide survey of 12, 000 senior managers, co-ordinated through *Harvard Business Review*, Peters (1991) suggests that managers are using the language of partnership but are thin on practice: 'There is a rhetoric of partnership in the business world today – and then there is the reality' (p. 98). It is difficult, for the practitioner as well as the researcher, to separate the two. The prescriptions are thin on how to effect the detail of the proposed revolution and are even weaker on intra-managerial politics (Wood, 1989).

However, they are reflecting on, and contributing to, an apparent shift in thinking about how organisations should be run and the ideology of management. One or more of the popular management books were frequently seen gracing the shelves of the offices occupied by the 'up and coming' generation of senior managers interviewed in our study, and the ideas introduced above were certainly part of the language used by our informants to explain their views on managing change.

This book is a contribution to analysing the real management activities which lie behind the easy prescriptions. Its substantive content is derived from a research project, funded by the Economic and Social Research Council and the Department of Trade and Industry, which explored the network of relationships between users and suppliers of computer technologies. Computer technologies were chosen because of their perceived centrality to improved business performance and because of their potential role in transforming the shape of the firm. Freeman (1986) argues that empirical findings on technical change point to the overwhelming importance of microelectronics as the basis of an emerging new paradigm of economic and innovative activity, where innovations have resulted in the very rare combination of a drastic fall in costs accompanied by the potential for massive improvements in technical performance across all sectors. The applications of such technical innovations are as yet under-developed. Regardless of whether the notion of a paradigm shift is accepted, it is clear that microelectronics products are for many firms an unknown quantity, in terms of both technical potential and significance for the firm's structure and division of labour. The focus of our study, however is not so much on the technologies as on the relationships between suppliers, users and their technical and managerial representatives. We start from the assumption that a key factor in both technical and social innovations by firms is the management of such relationships.

Whereas much earlier research has focused on the firm as the unit of analysis, we concentrate on the interface between two or more businesses, situating the firm in its market context. We analyse the business structures contrived to manage the uncertainties generated by product development and technology acquisition cycles. The roles of technical experts and senior and middle managers, as interest groups in the firm hierarchy and as agents directing significant capital investments, provide the substance of the research. The technologies studied were high-value products developed by specialist suppliers in the computing and instrumentation sectors for application to production and quality control processes or to be used as specialist tools for industrial research, product development and testing.

Our major aim is to explore the relationships between the development and marketing of computer technologies by suppliers and their use by customers. The empirical analysis focuses on two main areas. First, the implications of the type of relationship between supplier and customer for the development and use of computer products. The organisational arrangements are examined through analysis of the roles of technical experts and senior managers. Second, within supplier and customer firms, we identify those specialist groups who are instrumental in defining technical problems and providing possible solutions. We examine the potentially conflicting roles of such technical experts as inter-firm mediators of policy on the development or acquisition of technology and as negotiators of adaptation and innovation within and between firms.

INTER-FIRM RELATIONSHIPS AND ORGANISATIONAL STRUCTURE

The main themes underlying much of the contemporary discussion of management can in fact be expressed in terms of change along two dimensions or continua: first, organisational structures, and second, inter-organisational relationships. Our research is structured around these two themes.

The structural dimension characterises the division of labour and managerial style in the firm. We derive a broad distinction between organisation structures from Burns and Stalker's classic book *The Management of Innovation*. They suggested that organisations could be classified along a spectrum between mechanistic and organic forms. Mechanistic structures have a hierarchic control system, specialised differentiation of functions, and a vertical chain of authority, emphasising the disciplined obedience of subordinates to the decisions of superiors. In Weberian terms, a stable hierarchy promotes acceptance of legitimate authority and resolves problems of co-ordination and command. This structure is generally treated as appropriate for firms operating in a stable market. Expertise would tend to be functionally defined, but barriers between functions generally hinder open discussion and block the exchange of knowledge between specialisms. Intra-managerial conflict and 'empire building' may become the norm. The result is likely to be a slow, or inadequate, response to changes in product markets and considerable difficulty if continuous innovation is required. Organic structures, commonly associated with 'professional' forms of work, are meant to overcome some of these problems and hence to provide a structure appropriate to firms operating in unstable markets, where continuing innovation is a requirement for success. They are network based and rely heavily on the use of individual discretion at all levels. Fixed job content is replaced by continual adjustment of job tasks through interaction with others in cross-functional project teams. This is combined with an internalised commitment to the concern which goes beyond contractual obligations. The network structure of control means that authority is derived not from formal status but from expert knowledge. In a true organic system, the reward structure should reinforce contribution to the wider objectives of the firm, rather than strict performance of prescribed duties. In reality, of course, aspects of both structures may coexist within a firm with different occupational groups subject to different forms of control: firms with a mechanistic production control structure may operate with loose, organic forms for specialised professional groups such as research and development (R&D).

Second, we treat organisations as inter-linked through bargaining and influence networks, where an important aspect of the senior management role is the development of the necessary expertise for handling the range of supply chain relationships. We distinguish between such relationships in terms of a range from adversarial to collaborative. To the extent that firms are experimenting with more organic structures, the roles of managers and technical specialists are also likely to change: 'in the emerging organisation managers add value by deal making, by brokering at interfaces. . . . As managers and professionals spend more time working across boundaries with peers and partners over whom they have no direct control, their negotiating skills become essential assets' (Kanter, 1989, p. 89). We examine the reality of such bargaining and influence structures in operation.

It would be naive to assume that most negotiating relationships are collaborative: concern with purchasing efficiency, or in other words price, continues to dominate most supply chain exchanges, with adversarial tactics the norm. The adversarial style is market mediated and based on a zero-sum notion of profits and costs. It is typical of arrangements for buying products or processes which are well defined and understood. The adversarial form is based on short-term commitment and a simple price bargain; contractual arrangements are formally stipulated, delivery timetables are likely to be pre-defined and penalty clauses written into the supply contract. The buyer has to resolve any uncertainties about requirements internally (user needs and problems would be pre-defined and suppliers would have matched these with solutions). The only remaining uncertainty is the price of the good and the adversarial mode is well adapted to such quantitative flexibility. Bargaining is concerned with extracting concessions from the opposite party, horse-trading, bluff and counter bluff and saving face (or how to concede without appearing to). Bargainers may use a range of devices to extract information about the other's real position, while seeking to conceal their own bottom line. This kind of bargaining could also prevail in circumstances where the applications of a technology are ill defined but the user firm, using its own skilled people in a systems group for example, has been able to resolve the uncertainties internally. Adversarial bargaining is increasingly under attack for encouraging suppliers to cut quality in order to hold prices down, the end result being poorer goods and loss of competitiveness (Carlisle and Parker, 1989).

In contrast, an integrative bargaining model underlies much of the writing concerned with active management of the supply chain. In this scenario a buyer seeks to collaborate with suppliers, treating the bargain as non-zero sum. The development of a reciprocal partnership is based on a shared belief that cost control, quality and profit are mutually compatible. Not surprisingly this is hard to attain after many years of adversarial bargaining and its associated distrust. The collaborative model requires relatively open exchange of information between the customer and the supplier about user needs and problems. Contractual arrangements are likely to be more flexibly defined, but collaboration necessitates a longer-term mutual commitment which militates against financial flexibility in the user, such as changing orders in the light of market reversals. The language is one of partnership, strategic alliances, team work, open communication of needs, recognition of mutual interdependence and the need for respect (Burt, 1989; Carlisle and Parker, 1989). All of which sounds highly desirable, until one recalls that commercial contracts, competition between firms and profit are the substance of such partnerships. We explore the extent to which negotiating relationships fit these ideal types, or vary between the two. We also ask whether internal organisation structures affect the preferred style of negotiation. Is it, for example, feasible to combine a mechanistic structure with partnership styles of negotiation? We would predict that such a firm would be wedded to the adversarial style because it would have specialist buyers rewarded for performance on short-term price/cost, not on long-term advances in the relationship or in the quality of the goods supplied.

Research design and methodology

Our research is broadly ethnographic in approach, although we were constrained by the extent of access available to us as outsiders observing commercially sensitive transactions. The main case studies are based on three firms, two large multinationals and one medium-sized company. A programme of intensive interviewing was carried out with senior managers and technical experts in each of these, generating a number of cases of specific technology acquisitions and/or new product developments. Some interviews were carried out in other firms, linked to the main companies by virtue of the supply chain relationship. Most of the material was gathered over a two-year period between October 1988 and October 1990.

The most important research tool was the semi-structured interview, typically lasting between forty-five minutes and an hour and a half. The interview schedule was a point of departure rather than an end in itself: the objective was to allow the interviewee as much freedom as possible to define what was relevant to the line of questioning. Since we wanted to analyse the informal and the tacit aspects of user–supplier relations, as well as the more public face of contracting, semi-structured interviewing was the most appropriate technique. When requested, copies of the schedule were forwarded to informants prior to the interview. All interviews were tape-recorded and fully transcribed. These were then sent to interviewees for comments and further elaboration. Those interviewed ranged from senior management to shopfloor personnel, but there was a strong bias towards middle and senior managers, technical experts involved in product development and R&D, and sales representatives. We were successful in gaining privileged access to one fieldwork site, where a piece of observational research on the product development process was conducted. The fieldwork was carried out with the product development group of a manufacturer of high-capacity disk drives for original equipment manufacturer (OEM) computer firms, and concerned the role of suppliers and customers in the development process. A high level of observation was possible, including shadowing the product development manager, attending project meetings, and following transactions as they unfolded.

The three central firms, and the main technologies or acquisitions associated with them, were as follows.

Albion Spirits (AS) plc

Albion Spirits (AS), as its name implies, is a medium-sized company producing a range of beverages for the British and international markets. Shortly before we began to work there, it had been subjected to an acrimonious and politically sensitive takeover, the consequences of which were still rumbling on throughout the fieldwork period. A series of managers, technical experts and shopfloor supervisors were interviewed. Particular attention was paid to the organisational history of relationships between the engineering function, R&D laboratory and a newly created information services function set up after the takeover. A considerable body of material was obtained on the wide-ranging reforms that followed the takeover, when an attempt was made to pull a collection of largely autonomous brand-name companies into a single business unit. The fieldwork centred on the attempted standardisation of systems acquisition and development, the role played by the information services function and the management of external suppliers. In particular, we examined specific purchases, both retrospectively and in real time, to look at the relationship between the acquisition of new systems and organisational restructuring. Current technology policies were assessed in the light of the preoccupation of senior managers with using particular information technologies as an instrument of organisational change. We looked in detail at the part external relationships played in these changes. For example the supplier portfolio changed from a collaborative, long-term relationship with a single major supplier to a more confrontational set of relationships with a number of competing suppliers; there was a project to centralise supply chain management by means of information technology (IT) systems, and business policy aimed to increase the use of external sources of expertise (consultants, supplier personnel, etc.) instead of developing all systems expertise internally. These issues were examined specifically in relation to the following technical acquisitions:

1 an automatic process control system for a distillery, which formed the pilot for a common process control system;
2 a laboratory analysis management information system for R&D;
3 an automated plant maintenance system for a distillery, again forming a pilot for a common system;
4 a financial management system for the head office, which formed the pilot for the introduction of common financial systems across the company.

Telewave Electronics

The second central study was a British division of a US multinational corporation, Telewave Electronics (TE). It houses a regional sales team dealing in TE computer systems products and a specialised sales team concentrating on instrumentation. The division manufactures computer-based test and measurement systems and has in-house R&D and marketing teams. Interviewing was carried out in each of these business units. The interviews carried out with TE personnel were evenly split between R&D, sales and marketing staff. Additional interviews took place in another TE computer systems sales office. Detailed work was done on the organisational history of the plant, the changing pattern of relationships between sales, marketing and R&D departments, the product development cycle, sales strategies, relationships with users, and the nature and effectiveness of feedback loops designed to channel user experiences into product development. This work involved the detailed reconstruction of the development history of specific products and product enhancements, the collecting of material on particular user relationships where we also had accounts from the user side, such as Defence Electronics and Albion Spirits, and detailed work on the development of collaborative sales strategies.

Midas plc

Midas was a computer disk-drive manufacturer based in Britain, with some development facilities in the USA and its main manufacturing in the Far East. The UK engineering manager was prepared to allow a shadowing exercise, and access to product development meetings was agreed. All Midas (UK) development engineers and managers were interviewed. For a period of four months one of us shadowed the engineering manager for one day a week. Ongoing product developments, which were three different disk drives, were accompanied longitudinally over a period of nine months, and past product developments were reconstructed. Particular attention was paid to the management of expertise in electronic engineering, and the question of how the technical parameters of product development were set. The relationships between Midas and its suppliers and main customers were examined. Midas was a designated supplier to a major workstation manufacturer that was taken over by TE during the fieldwork period.

In addition to these firms, a number of others provided supplementary detail on supplier–user relations. First, material was collected on the organisation of sales, marketing and product development in Defence Electronics' (DE) telecommunications operating division. Defence Electronics is an important, long-standing customer for TE. We were therefore able to gain some insight into this highly specialised supplier–user relationship. Second, interviews were carried out with the sales representative, project manager and general manager of Smith Instruments & Engineering. This company supplied the automatic process control equipment to AS. A body of general material on relationships with users and the organisation of sales was also collected. Third, material concerned with the organisation of sales and marketing, and relationships with users was collected from Wax Systems. Wax Systems was the established, long-term supplier of computer systems to AS prior to takeover.

Apart from the case studies, contextual and documentary material was gathered from industry conferences and interviews with people well placed to give a strategic overview of the computer systems supply industry and the problems faced by users. They included trainers and consultants, representatives from the Department of Trade and Industry and Scottish Enterprise, local government, technology transfer institutes, and academics. Many of them recounted episodes and experiences which contributed to our stock of knowledge about real-world business practices and problems – and even occasional successes. In the chapters that follow, we draw upon this material intensively. Unlike the airport textbooks, we do not promise solutions to organisational problems. But we do think that, by grounding our analysis in an ethnography of business practice, we are not committing the sin of minimising the difficulties inherent in the management of change. We have tried to write something that will interest not just our colleagues, but the world-weary, enthusiastic, young, old, cynical, naive, ruthless, altruistic men and women, managers, scientists and experts to whom we owe a great deal of this book.

2   Experts and expertise

THE SOCIAL CONSTRUCTION OF EXPERTISE

The expert, along with the manager, is what much of this book is about. We decided to concentrate on them because of the central role they play both in the academic literature on organisational change and in the minds of those business people whose job it is to manage that change. Unpacking and interpreting social constructions of expertise may sound like an academic exercise with little direct relevance to those who manage organisations. In fact, it is linked in a very concrete way to the world of business problems and solutions. The social construction of expertise provides a bridge between the mental world of models and meanings, which are shared by groups of people, and the material world of innovation and business transactions. Social constructions of IT expertise, for example, cannot be interpreted without some knowledge of the concrete technologies to which they refer: software development, hardware platforms, digital signalling networks and so forth. Researchers need to understand the interrelationship between the material events and processes of the business world and the mental categories and models used to map that world by the groups who operate within it. In the same way as archaeologists interpret an artefact by looking at both its finished form and the raw materials that went into it, we need to understand that if social construction is the finished cultural product, the material world provided the raw material: we cannot look at the one without the other.

There are a number of contextual factors contributing to the perceived importance of managing expertise. The most pervasive of these is the notion that Western economies are changing from industrial to knowledge based, and that the ability of any nation state to maintain the status of advanced economy will depend increasingly on the appropriation of knowledge and its translation into saleable commodities. At the level of the firm, there is increasing awareness of the value of firm-specific, or contingent, knowledge, from shopfloor to management. This is allied with the increasing rate of incorporation of applied science into industry and the service sector, via professions such as industrial engineering and, increasingly, electrical and electronic engineering. Knowledge is incorporated into capital goods such as computer systems, and organisational practices are also the focus of codified knowledge via the management sciences. There is a growing economics of knowledge, concerned with such issues as organisational learning and problem-solving and the economic development and embodiment of knowledge, exemplified in the work of Nelson and Winter (1982) and Dosi (1984).

The more technologically complex an industrial sector becomes, the more expertise is treated as the lifeblood of the industry, not just in the obvious sense that it generates the innovations upon which growth depends, but because it circulates between companies in a constant flow of formal and informal transactions. To analyse and understand how expertise is managed by looking only at the internal dynamics of the firm would be as unrealistic as attempting to understand the human body by dissecting a single organ. The concept of expertise then highlights the need to focus on the social relations involved in designing technologies, making them work, using, adapting and perhaps discarding them. The engineers, sales managers, end-users, finance directors and others involved may be employed by different organisations but linked by a formal supply chain governed by commercial contracts and market styles of exchange. These exchanges may be mediated by outside experts from agencies in the public or the private sector. Alongside the formal market relationships, however, are informal networks mediating the exchange of knowledge, where personal friendships and professional associations between peers cut across company loyalties. The different interest groups typically have unequal status and skills, which will be reflected in the structural solutions devised to manage their transactions. The more esoteric the specialised knowledge possessed by the experts, the stronger the bonds of shared interest that link practitioners and the more freely information tends to circulate through trade journals and professional conferences, irrespective of the commercial rivalries between companies. In any case such technical experts often have considerable occupational mobility between firms, exploiting the opportunities available in exclusive labour markets where demand is high. We argue throughout this book that new divisions of expertise are in part the result of managerial attempts to control labour and other costs. This allows us to focus on the creation, and dissolution, of specialisms, and the shaping of divisions within management. It allows us to treat the management of change as a political process, not simply a functional problem about the efficient division of tasks and the integration of the business competencies of top management with the systems knowledge of technical experts.

The definition is sociological in orientation: expertise is treated as the expression of intertwined power relations, formal knowledge and experience-based know-how, within the framework of a capitalist economy. It allows for the substantive content of formal training and education, but asserts that formal knowledge and skills become expertise only when they are enacted through organisation structures, which are the forum for experiential learning and give direction to formal knowledge. In this sense an engineering graduate, for example, develops expertise when he or she applies formal knowledge in a specific technical context, such as product development, which is in turn defined by the management policies and practices of the firm. Such organisation structures make some forms of argument and procedures for technical decisions legitimate, while excluding others, and allocate different specialist groups to unequal statuses.

For analytical purposes it is possible to separate expertise into different components. It can, for example, be characterised as located in the individual who develops expertise through a combination of formal knowledge and specific experience of the socio-technical context in the firm. People may benefit psychologically from the pleasure derived from the use of such skills, or may be disempowered by their experience of a management structure which controls their discretion and work activities. Because the deployment of expertise is fundamentally concerned with power relations between, and within, management specialisms and skilled labour, it is not freely developed and exchanged, but is embedded within management control structures (Fleck and Tierney, 1991). Crucially, these are likely to define some groups as skilled and as able to exercise their skills, with due recognition of status, while other groups are discounted. This is often the position of women clerical workers, for example, who may be instrumental in making new office systems workable, but who are generally not rewarded by improved formal status. Most of the public roles commonly defined as expert in character are dominated by men. Women frequently occupy interstitial roles, which require them to handle communication between the diverse male-dominated interest groups involved in the management of computer systems. Hence they acquire a degree of technical know-how, but generally have limited control over new systems development (Cockburn, 1985). Thus there is always a political element in definitions of skill and expertise.

MANAGING EXPERTISE IN ORGANISATIONS

Because expertise is socially constructed and changes over time, its management is extremely problematic. All firms, however well established, have to anticipate and manage change. They operate under conditions of uncertainty: patterns of demand change over time in ways that firms can rarely fully control, technologies evolve or are displaced by successive innovations, the availability and market price of particular skills changes, established competitors alter their product lines and marketing strategies, new competitors may enter the market and there will be fluctuations in the wider economy. The general level of business activity is conditioned by macroeconomic variables, such as commodity prices and interest rates, themselves dependent on political events and social trends. Even the senior managers of the most powerful multinationals can neither predict nor fully control such factors. An equally rich set of uncertainties are internal to the firm: can the product be designed and manufactured to the timescales and within the budget set by management; are there any features likely to cause problems once manufacturing begins; are senior management's perceptions of market demands and setting of profit margins reasonable; what marketing strategies would be most appropriate, and, most crucially, how many will sell, and what price will the customer be prepared to pay?

At each stage from the drawing board to the marketplace, the essence of the manager's job is the reduction of these uncertainties. The most important function of specialised knowledge and procedures within the firm is to minimise the uncertainties that attend each stage of the production process, as well as the external uncertainties that come into play once the product (and/or the service) is released onto the market. A parallel set of processes can be described in the user firms who comprise the market for ICT suppliers. Here expertise is needed to manage the interface with suppliers; expert groups play a key role in internal systems development, negotiating budgets and contracts, controlling costs and timetables, and making the systems run. The word used by managers to denote the processes of charting the way through uncertainties on both sides of the user–supplier relationship is 'strategy'.

The getting, cultivation and deployment of expertise pose crucial questions for managers, all of which are at the heart of 'business strategy' and the conditioning of relationships between firms. The most obvious issues within the firm concern the recruitment, training, salary structure and promotion systems for experts. The latter is particularly significant for the relationship between senior management and expert groups, and determines the extent to which technical experts move into management. At the same time, in most companies different forms of expertise are likely to be organised under broad functional headings: R&D, manufacturing, marketing, sales and so forth. From a management perspective the weight given to each in the setting of strategy and the allocation of resources is a pre-eminent political issue within firms. If the timescales for the definition of a new product are driven predominantly by marketing considerations, for example, development engineers will often feel they are unrealistic because technical constraints have not been given their proper weight. On the other hand, if the 'research' part of R&D is given a disproportionate voice in product development, they may lose sight of commercial objectives entirely:

> The old way of doing things . . . [was] you discovered that you could do something better and . . . made a product out of it, and then found out if people wanted to buy it!
>
> (Salesperson, Telewave Electronics)

The social construction of expertise does not just encompass the defining of who the experts are, how expertise is acquired and passed on and the nature of creativity and innovation; it also revolves around appropriate ways experts are to be managed. This means that electronic engineers, to take a concrete example, can resort to an arsenal of widely shared social beliefs about the management of experts to buttress their position within firms whenever they feel it threatened. A management attempting to supervise and closely direct qualified electronic engineers will encounter a great deal of resistance if it fails to take this into account:

> Because we've got a lot of technically and professionally qualified people, they don't need a lot of detailed supervision very often. . . .
>
> (Section head, R&D, TE)

An important part of the professionalisation of expertise is to do with the ascription of responsibility, with experts being assumed to have the capacity to organise their own work schedules and work without close supervision. In areas where innovation is highly valued, such as product development, experts may refer to an equally powerful body of beliefs about the nature of creativity and appropriate ways to encourage its flowering – many of which have to do with the importance of giving experts control over their own timetables and not imposing standards of dress, behaviour and communication skills that apply elsewhere in the organisation. This creates problems for managerial control, because in a profit-centred organisation allowing experts too much autonomy interferes with profit-making, as market considerations are edged out by fascination with technical investigation. Lack of close supervision, for example, is widely construed as integral to creativity and innovation. In the example below it had a commercial pay-off, but it would be easy to imagine disastrous outcomes as well.

> One of the best, most profitable products we have got, I championed here to begin with without any official sanction . . . I won't bore you with the technical details . . . this first product had very limited possibilities for sales . . . but we realised in doing it that there was a different way of

meeting a slightly different aspect of the requirement in a much better way. So we did it as quickly as possible under the bench and got the thing to the point where it looked feasible, and then said, can we do it? And somebody, my R&D manager at the time, said yes, I suppose you'd better do it, so we went off and finished it. . . . I think there's a kind of understanding in Telewave that provided you're not under intense business pressure and you're not in trouble, everybody should be allowed just a little bit going on under the bench.

(Section head, R&D, Telewave Electronics)

This issue of the control and motivation of expert labour has been analysed at greatest length in a body of academic work known as labour process theory. Within this tradition, recent debate has centred on the use by managers of the apparently opposing strategies of direct control versus responsible autonomy. In an extensive study of computer systems development, Friedman and Cornford (1989) extend this terminology to the management of systems engineers. They conclude tentatively that there was no single solution to the effective management of such staff, but that a form of 'managed autonomy' was the most common form in current use. By this they mean that relatively *laissez-faire* styles of management appeared to be giving way to more formal control systems, albeit within a framework which gives considerable discretion to the engineers. Armstrong (1984) adopts a slightly different perspective, arguing that professional groups struggle to lay claim to an area of expertise over which they can maintain sole control. His study of accountants, personnel managers and engineers explores the relative success of these groups in claiming exclusive rights over the practice of specific techniques as a means to collective upward mobility. This analysis is extended in a discussion of the agency relationship between owners or employers and managers: management is treated as a relationship based either on trust or on performance monitoring and control as substitutes for trust. Trusting senior managers, and their subordinate manager-agents, to uphold the interests of owners and shareholders is expensive in terms of salary levels and life styles, but appears indispensable. There is therefore a financial incentive for employers to replace trust with monitoring and control. Because of this contradiction, emergent technical and managerial specialisms try to lay claim to trust and its privileges, while reducing the employer's need to trust existing specialists. Armstrong (1989) sees emergent specialisms (such as systems analysts) as offering new partial solutions 'to the agency problem faced by owners. The more incomprehensible (to outsiders) the techniques possessed by the specialist group, the higher the price that group is able to command for its skills. Experts wield power to the extent that they are able to define, and control, an area of uncertainty; they lose power to the extent that resolution of that uncertainty becomes a matter of routine.

In these terms, we should expect expert groups to have different statuses and degrees of autonomy and privilege depending on their relationship to owners, shareholders and senior management. Where they are part of managerial work, their status should depend on their ability to offer a new monitoring or control solution to the problem of trust. A contemporary example of this would be the development of management information systems. Experts may also be regarded as a device inserted into organisational hierarchies during periods of change, to legitimise managers' preferred technical solutions, and to defuse the potential grievances of those groups who are the target of changes detrimental to them. The insertion of technical specialists may be a tactic used when managers seek to avoid open negotiation over the organisational and work-related changes envisaged with the introduction of new technology. The strategy may of course have unpredictable consequences. If the expert group is able to maintain exclusive control over its knowledge, it becomes inherently difficult to manage and there is a constant danger that it will begin to operate independently. On the other hand, where experts are part of productive labour, as in the case of development engineers, they may be subject to a variety of direct control strategies, including deskilling and the codification of their knowledge. Ironically, one of the consequences of the increasing pace of innovation in modern ICTs is the greater pace at which expertise becomes redundant. Now more than ever, expertise must be constantly renewed: this sometimes gives managers a tactical advantage.

From the point of view of management, the struggle between autonomy and control is a double-edged sword. Managers often rely on the fact that experts will put in the concentrated effort needed to solve technical problems without regard to the time involved. Conversely the notions which experts share about professional autonomy, and the appropriate managerial attitudes towards supervision, are always a potential or actual management problem. Within every company – and within many public sector organisations – there are grey areas where managers and experts both feel that their remits within the organisation entitle them to make decisions. These grey areas can be thought of at one level as a kind of conceptual battleground, where social constructions of management and of expertise overlap. The grey areas are made up of the overlaying of technical decision-making, which belongs to the domain of specialised knowledge that is the expert's traditional territory, with the organisational, strategic considerations which management regards as its prerogative. Grey areas, it goes without saying, are a major problem in the management of uncertainty. They generate doubts and ambiguities which impede not merely the internal cohesion of the firm but also the construction of the type of external relationships which enable it to manage change effectively.

Problematic though grey areas are, they are also relatively predictable. They cluster around the specific arenas which bring experts and managers into intensive contact. For analytical purposes these arenas can be divided into three and treated separately. The most important we shall call strategic policymaking; revolving around that, and to some degree dependent upon it, are skills policies and technology policies.

Strategic policymaking

A significant proportion of what managers define as strategic questions explicitly concern expertise. Business planning involves the setting of priorities and objectives to do with the skills base within the company, the technology to be acquired, the relationships with major suppliers and the setting of the balance between internal and external sources of expertise. The decisions surrounding strategic policies have a rich potential for conflict between managers and experts, since in practice it is difficult to draw the line between their respective responsibilities.

In the case of ITs, strategic policymaking is to a large extent based on perceptions of technical trends or likely future innovations relevant to company operations. Telecommunications network technologies in the late 1980s and early 1990s, to take one example, underwent a transition from analogue to digital signalling which forced rapid change on the skills base necessary to maintain competitiveness, for both suppliers of telecommunications technology and its users. Technical experts may regard themselves as better qualified than managers to predict trends and draw strategic conclusions from them, especially as this policymaking underlies technology acquisition, one of their core preoccupations. Experts may also have strong opinions on the existing skills base within the company, and how it needs to be adjusted or improved: they may be committed to one supplier or particularly hostile to a possible external source of expertise. If such issues are not successfully addressed by managers, the grey areas in strategic policymaking result in parallel struggles for control over decision-making in core areas of company operations.

Skills policies

Decisions about the composition of the skills base within companies are most directly reflected in practices of recruitment, training and retraining, and redundancy. The recruitment of experts can be a fertile source of conflict, with experts concerned primarily with technical competence and managers often seeking to add business-oriented recruitment criteria. Company experts, like this head of a research laboratory in Albion Spirits (AS), can be extremely hostile to the imposition of non-technical criteria on the recruitment of specialists – understandably, since it represents an overt threat not just to his organisational fiefdom but also to his capacity to define the type of work which is done within the laboratory, the core responsibility of the technical specialist:

> We are also now very heavily into this graduate recruitment business, bringing in the whizz kids and they get hurtled round the place at a great rate of knots for about nine months . . . so their feet hardly touch the ground. . . . So one of the throw-outs from that is, what's the difference between the people recruited from that scheme and people who are recruited sort of piecemeal during the year? In other words, if you bring a chemist in through that scheme, and you train a chemist in here to do a specific job, is the chap who is brought in to do the specific job here a second-class citizen rather than a first-class chemist? . . . Is he going to have the same career opportunities put in front of him in his obviously less high profile situation because these management recruits are being shot round the place and meeting all sorts of people, having cocktails with chief executives and all that?

Training and retraining policies are also a core preoccupation for technical specialists. Conflicts fall into two main types: struggles over the definition of the optimal skills base within the company or department, which belong to the realm of strategic policymaking, and more detailed struggles over training regimes. The larger the company, the more formally structured training tends to be, with a formal induction process and regular courses updating technical knowledge in established areas of expertise or introducing new ones. One reason for the very low turnover of experts in Telewave Electronics, for example, where many scientists had joined the company fresh from university and stayed with it throughout their working lives, was the way Telewave offered regular training, often in other countries, and retraining in other specialist areas if appropriate to business strategy. On the other hand, training policies in smaller companies can be extremely problematic, especially when the technologies in question are complex and the pace of innovation is swift. Ironically experts may find themselves hoist on their own petard, when they find that one of the consequences of the belief that experts can quickly absorb new knowledge and techniques is that recent graduates arriving in firms with little or no experience are thrown in at the deep end, and left to sink or swim.

A less obvious but equally important aspect of skills policies is what might be called the question of redundant expertise. The nature of innovation is that it makes certain branches of expertise redundant, and experts can find themselves falling behind the pace of change. When managers find themselves thinking of headcounts and cost cutting, experts are no less vulnerable than other categories of worker. An inevitable result of change in a company's skills base, especially if retraining is a low priority, is that certain areas of expertise, and, more to the point, certain experts, become surplus to requirements. Equally, companies may well decide to follow a strategy of running down the internal skills base and contracting in expertise when required. The balancing act between make or buy can itself generate problems: the advantage of internal sources of expertise is that managers can set the terms of reference far more easily than they can when dealing with external experts, where a level of dependence on the supplier is inevitable.

Technology policies

One of the most commonly encountered disputes between experts and managers centres around the tension in technology acquisition between function and application. Few things are as important to experts as the systems, instruments and development tools they work with. The participation of management in the setting of technology policies can be perceived by experts as an intrusion. In questions of technology, irrespective of whether the company is primarily a user or a supplier of ICTs, there is a tendency for the technical expert to focus more narrowly on function, on engineering features like capacity, power and response time. Managers, on the other hand, will worry that specialists are losing sight of applications, and wonder whether 'a box with all the bells and whistles' is strictly necessary for what may be a relatively mundane application.

In making purchasing decisions, managers also introduce considerations which constrain technical decisions in a way experts will view as unreasonable. Sometimes the reason is cost, but more often it centres around strategic policymaking, such as questions of compatibility between different systems. Equally, the purchasing decision is itself part of an internal political process, and symbolises the status and power of one group *vis-à-vis* another. Rather than being a technical decision, based on standardised procedures comparing equipment performance, managers seek to widen the purchasing criteria. In particular, they are likely to consider the relationship with the supplier, how it fits into the desired supplier portfolio, and the implications the purchase is likely to have for the internal skills base. Managers may have internal political reasons for blocking the purchase of particular tools, or they may not want to purchase a piece of equipment from a given supplier, even if experts are convinced they need it: they may not wish to enter into a relationship with a particular supplier, or require technology to be acquired from a number of suppliers to cut costs and increase responsiveness by playing them off against each other. What experts may view as a relatively straightforward process, where performances are compared and purchasing decisions are made on a rational combination of function and cost considerations, in fact turns out to be part of a great game being played by senior management, where political and economic imperatives are if anything more important than purely technical considerations.

Computer technologies and expertise

The development and control of computer technologies and systems has become a critical area for 'expert management'. Although the market is too multilayered for generalisations to be easy, it is certainly the case that since the 1950s function has on the whole gradually been losing out to application as the most important determinant of purchasing decisions. Managers tend to be considerably more in control of purchases in the 1990s than they were in the 1950s and 1960s, as one would expect in a market where the balance of knowledge has shifted in favour of users.

The maturing of markets has resulted in changes in the definition of expertise unanticipated even by such acute analysts of business life as Burns and Stalker. All markets in technically complex products see a shift in focus from function to application over time and an associated change in what could be called the balance of expertise between producers and users. In the early days of a technology, immediately after it enters the marketplace and users learn how to operate it, the balance of knowledge is lopsided. The producer has much greater familiarity with the technical characteristics of the innovation, and innovators will also have had the opportunity to develop their thinking about potential applications before users. In addition, there are various ways in which producers can try to institutionalise their lead, such as producing proprietary operating systems which attempt to lock users into a particular supplier and/or regularly updating product lines.

As users gain experience, the balance of knowledge becomes more equitable: users become more familiar with the technical questions centring around function and start to explore applications more systematically. Finally, as the market becomes mature, the balance of knowledge turns against the original producers of the innovation, with thoroughly experienced users and a number of skilled third parties, such as software development houses, becoming alternative sources of expertise for users to turn to. The direct, perhaps highly collaborative, contact between an innovating company and the customer, which characterised the early phase of market development, may become much more adversarial, with big customers threatening to take their business elsewhere if they do not receive better service.

The market for computer products, as with many other technologies, can be seen as a composite of a large number of sub-markets in different industrial and service sectors. In each of these technological innovation plays a pivotal role in the manoeuvres between innovators and users. Increasingly self-confident users move along the learning curve that leads through concern with technical function towards familiarity with applications. Meanwhile, innovators are striving to return the balance of knowledge in their favour, usually by product enhancements and the updating of product lines. From the user's perspective this often seems more an attempt to move the goalposts of the supplier relationship than a response to a real market need. Occasionally the innovator manages to rewrite the rulebook altogether, coming up with a radical advance which replaces a mature market in an established product with a highly immature market in a new product, thus allowing innovators some breathing space before the balance of knowledge shifts towards users once again.

In the first wave of computerisation, suppliers were concerned with capacity and performance of systems. They were developing and marketing 'boxes' with equipment-based processing power inside them. Their organisations were R&D oriented with sales as a mediatory body. Users developed centralised data processing departments, based on mainframe computing and led by technical specialists who were often committed to one supplier. Technical experts and managers operated in separate spheres: there was relatively little managerial input into technical decision-making and, conversely, there was little technical input into the running of the company. The term 'data processing' is itself associated with the black-boxing of expertise: the drawing of a thick black line around what is seen as a body of technical knowledge so important that it has to be treated as a discrete aspect of company operations and dealt with on its own. 'Data processing' happened in its own department, where the technical specialist held sway. Suppliers dealt with data processing managers on an engineer-to-engineer basis. Inevitably, the data processing department subscribed to the expert-as-scientist construction of expertise, which is examined in more detail below. At the level of the firm, the result was a stress on internal over external sources of expertise. Programmers, for example, may well prefer to write their own applications rather than buy in software packages. If this happens on any scale in different data processing groups across the business, senior managers face major problems of compatibility and a lack of standardised system procedures.

In the second wave of computerisation, users have started to look for functionality in the systems. They expect to set their own standards and make greater demands on suppliers. Business managers want to use the technology as part of the strategic armoury of the firm: distributed processing is the buzz word. To effect such a change, the old data processing empires have to be dispersed and structures devised to create 'business-minded' technical experts, who put profit first and see themselves as servicing the end users rather than building their own ivory towers.

The increasing involvement of managers in technology purchasing decisions, together with the maturing of computer products and markets, has led to marked changes in the sales strategies used by suppliers, who are increasingly having to sell services and expertise rather than 'products'. In their terms they are no longer selling boxes, but diagnosing and solving business problems and 'adding value' to the customer's business. Structurally, senior management is likely to be concerned with making R&D more responsive to the marketplace through enforced liaison with marketing and manufacturing.

The result has been considerable change in the type of technologies most favoured by the marketplace and in the rhetoric of selling. The increasing focus on applications has been reflected, in broad terms, in the growth of distributed computing, where the most pressing technical issues are to do with compatibility: in other words, the hardware in itself becomes less important than the relationship between components of the system. Although minimum performance thresholds will be set by users, 'black boxes' are regarded as basically similar, and managers assign more strategic importance to the flow of information within and between organisation networks.

One of the underlying functional concerns in both user and supplier organisations is to build bridges between the knowledge specialisms of different groups and to draw on, and integrate, the tacit and contingent knowledge located within groups in order to make new products and systems work. If we treat the relationship between the shape of such systems and the distribution of expertise as simply a technical problem for management, concerned with resourcing the business, it is possible to outline a number of hypothetical structural solutions. Dyerson and Roper (1991) and Tierney and Williams (1991) provide successful and failed examples of these exercises in new systems development. The project team is probably the most common device used to manage the integration of the different sources of expertise and knowhow necessary to the establishment of the system. In the successful examples, such as the computerisation of PAYE reported by Dyerson and Roper, senior management used project teams to integrate the technical and project management expertise of external consultants with the internal understanding of system requirements and programming capabilities. End users, programmers and consultants were required to work alongside each other from the start. The aim was to use the superior skills of the highly paid consultants to 'train' in-house experts. Resentment about the high level of pay received by the consultants was restricted by ensuring that they always had skills which were not represented in-house.

Similar processes are reported in Tierney and Williams (1991) where collaboration between a small specialist software supplier and a large insurance firm was regarded as highly profitable all round. The supplier in this case used the customer as a case study for system development, but also subsequently paid royalties to the customer for their context-specific, knowledge-based contribution to the software. Other structural devices include the incorporation, or secondment, of technical specialists to business departments, or vice versa, and the secondment of end users to technical groups. Some end users may also begin to occupy new specialist quasi-technical roles, mediating between departments, senior managers and development engineers. It often seems to be women who fulfil these transitional roles, perhaps because they are perceived as being better at dealing with people and, tied up with this, non-threatening to the underlying male status quo. There may also be new elite groups of specialists who are treated as a 'flexible resource' to be allocated to projects at the behest of senior management, or specialists may be hived off to separate or subsidiary companies. Joint/collaborative ventures between firms may be experimented with, to the extent that they are perceived to limit the risk involved in investing in new technical directions. A much publicised example of such a strategic alliance was that between the French Groupe Bull and IBM, which gave Bull access to IBM's RISC (reduced instruction set computing) technology and IBM access to the French government market. In the longer term, this was expected to open up other new markets for RISC and stimulate Bull's development of symmetrical multi-processing, an advanced technique expected to have an important future role. All of these organisational devices may be supported (or undermined) by different reward and incentive schemes and different detailed divisions of labour between specialisms.

The above discussion would suggest that managing the combination of new technologies and expertise, in suppliers or users, is simply a matter of finding the correct structural solutions to fit the organisation for an era of continuous change. Let us muddy the water by putting power relations firmly in the centre. The switch in perspective means that expertise has to be seen not just as a business resource to be rationally allocated to tasks, but also as a source of power and status. As we shall see in the following chapters, the only way to make sense of the range of strategies deployed is to incorporate power relations into the analysis.

Changing definitions of the expert

The result of the tension between function and application in computer systems markets is that there is a striking lack of consensus when it comes to the management of expertise. Function and application provide mutually exclusive axes along which it is possible to order notions of expertise and define experts.

Those definitions of expertise which stress function over application are a sub-set of the wider and historically well-established classification of the expert as scientist, a person initiated via higher education and workplace training into a body of specialised knowledge and practices. Unlike other definitions, which stress flexibility and the capacity to absorb and act upon a range of different kinds of information, expertise is defined as such precisely because it is highly specialised, difficult to combine with other branches of knowledge, and comes encoded in a technical vocabulary which is impenetrable to non-initiates. In the vocabulary of sociology – often no less impenetrable to outsiders than the vocabulary of electronic engineering – specialisation implies a high degree of segmentation. Specialist knowledge is divided up into a large number of precisely defined fields, separated by disciplinary boundaries. Many technical experts, when asked what their field is, have to go into considerable detail, first identifying their broad disciplinary field – 'electronic engineering' – and then the particular sub-field in which they specialise – 'thermal engineering in disk-drive design'. Although boundaries between specialisations are not uncrossable, transferring from one field to another is seen as a demanding and time-consuming process, involving the absorption of a mass of complex technical information. According to this version, experts are defined as people working with a narrow but extremely detailed focus, in jobs which are highly segmented and have very clear boundaries. Outsiders, even those with a grounding in technical issues such as this project manager in AS, think of function-based expertise as 'technical' and therefore something of a mystery. Depending on the circumstances, this can give it a certain glamorous mystique or provoke deep suspicion and hostility:

> I tended always to take the view that you don't interfere with the technical side; you've got technicians to solve those [problems]. From a business point of view you know what you want to get out, you know what you want to put in, and as long as you are able to explain, this is what I want out, you can let them get on with the mechanics of it. . . . I've been almost taking it as the black box syndrome, seeing what goes in and what comes out and then understanding how it manipulates what's inside, but not getting too involved in the programming and the technical side.

The 'black box' defining of expertise is widely used in industrial societies to characterise scientists, who may in turn exploit such definitions of their work to guarantee funding and influence policymakers: the Strategic Defence Initiative in the USA was the largest-scale example of such special pleading, the socially constructed element of the exercise being made manifest in the Star Wars nickname. In the marketplace, however, the technical expert has to contend with more difficult opposition than gullible politicians provide. Company managers increasingly want to reject black box constructions of expertise in favour of managerial, applications-based doctrines which look outwards to the marketplace rather than inwards to the workstation. Their definitions of expertise are therefore likely to be radically different from function-based definitions. Where the black box notion of expertise stressed specialisation and profound knowledge of defined areas, an opposing school of thought, represented among contemporary managers, stresses flexibility and 'providing a service to the business' over depth of specialist knowledge, and refers to 'old-style' technical specialists disparagingly as 'techies'. This managerial definition of expertise is, quite literally, more businesslike. Expertise in technical function is seen as less important than expertise in managing applications to provide, for example, efficient IT services across the business, which deliver both the horizontal flow of information necessary for controlling operations and the vertical flow necessary for management decision-making. This in turn depends on stressing the expert's capacity to absorb a wide range of information of different types – not just 'engineering' or even 'scientific' information, but information to do with the full range of company operations – and to monitor relevant external variables (level of demand, economic indicators, technical trends, etc.). For example, there has been a significant redefinition of the 'computer systems expert', encapsulated in this comment by an AS manager in the process of radically restructuring what he regarded as outmoded skills within his company:

I emphasised to everybody . . . there's a tremendous opportunity here to make these people, to turn them from 60s or 70s based DP [data processing] professionals into 80s, 90s information systems professionals. So first of all it's in their interest, financially and in terms of the marketplace, to be *au fait* with the state of the art tools, whatever they are. It's also in our interests because it's the only way we can realistically hope to keep on top of that MIS [management information systems] circuit. . . . So I've given them the commitment that I'll reskill and redevelop as long as they recognise that they've got to change.

This 'expert' is a generalist rather than a specialist, a jack of all trades rather than master of one or two, capable of extracting the information most relevant to management decisions from a mass of operational detail, and then making both everyday operational decisions and longer-term 'strategic' analyses.

CONCLUSION

In a period of widespread questioning of conventional solutions to problems of efficiency and profitability, it is not just established expert groups and technical elites who are subject to new forms of control. The taken-for-granted bases of managerial authority are also being held up for scrutiny by employers, senior managers and competing expert groups, looking to improve the career chances of their own specialism. As Burns and Stalker (1961) demonstrated so vividly, the attempt to create more organic business structures, which appear to be adapted to periods of rapid change, is highly threatening to existing functional managers. Specialist managers, in the organisational control structure, and professionals, in occupational niches, are required to integrate their different types of expertise. The specialists, depending on the terms, may see this as an opportunity to gain the privileges of managerial status, or feel threatened because they may lose exclusive control over their knowledge. Many middle managers are likely to suspect their own long-term demise if they, in turn, are unable to demonstrate some exclusive skill. In the ideology of the organic firm, the manager can no longer rely on management by dictat. The role becomes one of co-ordinating different sources of expertise, with open access to shared information. Authority is derived from the exercise of recognised skills, not formal status. For most managers this offers a considerable threat to their identity, especially if they feel that their own relevant knowledge is inadequate. They may be uncertain about how to manage the apparent contradiction between giving autonomy to newly created project teams and trying to control their activities and limit their influence. At worst they may retreat into defensiveness, inhibiting the very changes they were meant to facilitate.

Throughout this century employers and managers have sought to develop belief systems which legitimate and sustain their right to authority over the workforce. In the 1920s, Taylorism and scientific management provided a new science-based rationale for growing numbers of middle managers whose authority came to rest on claims to the exclusive right to knowledge and information necessary for the control and planning of production. More recently, the management sciences, and their dissemination through business school degrees such as the MBA, have served as legitimising devices for new management specialisms. In the case of managerial expertise (and ironically in precisely the same way as other forms of expertise such as engineering, which may be the bane of the manager's working life), formal education and credentialling lend legitimacy to the manager's role as guardian of the most important organisational knowledge, and justify the exclusion of others from access. Managers then have a vested interest in resisting changes which seem to threaten the bases of their authority. When conventional managerial divisions of labour are being renegotiated and organisational hierarchies are themselves the focus of change, the dynamics of buying, selling and developing computer products and systems are likely to be highly charged: occupational identities, status and power underlie such transactions. In the next chapter, we see how issues relating to the management of expertise have a very direct impact on our case study companies.

3 The view from the supplier

Rhetoric and reality in responding to the market

Imagine for a moment that you are the managing director of an established supplier of computer technology. It doesn't matter which company or technology you choose, because the problems this chapter concentrates on cut across sub-markets to affect the sector as a whole. We shall be using three companies to exemplify the business of supplying such technologies, each of them very different, but you need not confine yourself to them. If you put yourself in the shoes of a managing director in the IT sector, what are you thinking in the 1990s? How does the future look? 'New wave' writers on business organisation suggest, amongst other things, the need for more collaborative, long-term relations between suppliers and customers as a means of improving business performance. What does this mean in practice for the organisation and management of product development?

Your first thought, as you mull over the way things were in the 1980s, is that things aren't what they used to be. The chances are your company grew much faster in the past than it is likely to in the future. Your market is an increasingly mature one, and the level of competition is much more intense than it was. You are especially fearful of competition from Japan, as the Japanese electronics industry moves into new high-technology areas such as test and measurement equipment, where you previously only had to contend with Western competitors. Even without the Japanese, you still face increasing competition from niche suppliers. As the market matures, small, highly specialised firms are concentrating on supplying narrow markets in particular sectors: it is increasingly difficult to maintain your dominant position even in traditional core markets.

At the same time, an important technological change is quickening the pace of innovation. One of the features of the 1980s was 'everything becomes computing', as digital information systems made enormous strides. Telephone systems, for example, are built around what engineers term signalling. Telephone networks used to be based on analogue signalling, where every voice or data call had a signalling channel associated with it to carry the message. Digital signalling technology developed in the 1980s, however, was able to codify signals into data streams consisting of ones and noughts. This allowed telephone networks to become computers talking to other computers through data links regulated by complex software protocols. Similarly, automatic process control machinery, used to monitor and control industrial processes in installations like distilleries and oil refineries, underwent the latest in a series of technological transformations in the 1980s with the production of digitally based process control systems. This is the fourth generation of instrumentation technology this century, as the basis of instruments shifted from hydraulic to pneumatic to electronic. The move towards digital signal processing (DSP) has significantly extended the domain of information technology, forcing established suppliers of process control instruments and telecommunications signalling test equipment, to name just two, to redefine their products, and the expertise they need to innovate, as computing. As a managing director you see opportunities to compensate for the maturing of old markets in the growth of new ones, but it won't be an easy option: DSP also means accepting and keeping up with a rapid pace of innovation, which in turn means developing or buying in expertise in expensive and often unfamiliar areas such as software development.

Partly as a result of increasing competition, which is itself both fuelling and fuelled by the pace of innovation within the IT sector, your product development cycles are getting shorter. Your marketing people are screaming they need Product X yesterday, your overworked but probably not underpaid development engineers are often under intense time pressure to complete projects, and your sales team, with more competitors to deal with, feels increasingly beleaguered. All in all, the working atmosphere in your company has probably gone downhill in the past few years. Paradoxically, despite the unprecedented pace at which products are hitting the marketplace, most people inside and outside your company think that there are fewer differences between your product line and those of your competitors than there have ever been. Users in particular are finding it harder to differentiate between suppliers on the technical characteristics of their products – a long-term development one would predict in mature markets. This has very direct implications for the way your products are presented to potential customers.

In other words, the market is putting you under considerable business pressure. If you keep a cool head, and you wouldn't have got to where you are today if you didn't, you know that you have to return to the basics: you must be responsive, you must be driven by customer needs and give the market what it wants, not what your R&D people think it needs. In the background you hear the supporting chorus from trade papers, business schools, industry seminars, government agencies, all of them saying the same thing – the way you give the market what it wants is by constructing feedback loops to channel the experience of users of products into the R&D lab, and specifically into the heads of R&D product development engineers. If you are a particularly literate managing director, you might even remember the story recounted by Burns and Stalker of the development of British radar technology in the early days of the Second World War, where electronic engineers were inspired to new heights of user-driven product innovation by having regular chances to talk to the radar controllers and fighter pilots whose lives often depended on the speed and efficiency of the product development cycle in the radar industry.

So, let us finally imagine that, fired with determination to supply the products customers want, you set out to design feedback loops leading from users into product development. You will immediately run into problems, some practical, some conceptual, but all of them potentially fatal. First, how do you define your user? This is not as obvious as it sounds: it is not just a customer company but a user within that company, anybody from a manager to an engineer to a shopfloor worker. How do you decide who you are selling to if, as is often the case, the 'user' is not the person who negotiates the sale with the supplier? Things can get even more complicated. In large suppliers with wide-ranging products, those involved in product development may not even get close to a customer, end-user or otherwise: they have to deal first with a sales force who have to be convinced to sell this specific part of the product range rather than any other. In a very real sense product development is driven internally, with R&D in effect 'selling' a product to a sales force, not an external user.

Then there is the point that words like feedback, market reaction and customer experience have vague meanings: they cover a multitude of different ways in which experience can be transmitted, and a number of different places within the supplier it can be channelled to. Sales and marketing departments have standardised procedures, but there are a number of less formal, structured routes along which experience and opinions flow between suppliers and customers, as we shall see. If routes of feedback vary, the content can vary even more, which itself poses problems: an electronic engineer working in product development may want a particular piece of technical information on equipment performance, which the salesperson may not have the specialist expertise either to ask for or to pick up on when it is volunteered. While it may be relatively easy to design an enhancement to an existing product on the basis of user desires, it is much more difficult to get substantive feedback on a new product before it enters the marketplace. Technical experts within suppliers point out that customers respond with generalising wish-lists when asked what they want, and very rarely with the kind of detailed response which can form the basis for a dialogue about technical features and potential applications. Even more serious is the fact that customer feedback rarely contains the most vital information for a supplier thinking of a new product: the price customers would be prepared to pay, and the potential size of the market.

Finally, from your viewpoint as managing director, there are two basic problems with users, however defined: they don't always agree, and what they want is sometimes technically stupid. It sounds straightforward enough when you hear somebody talking, as you often do, about the need for suppliers to be responsive to market needs, so you devote considerable effort through your marketing department to find out what those needs are. Inevitably, you find customer opinion is far from monolithic: there is a divergence of views, as is only to be expected from firms in different economic sectors facing a wide range of business problems. In an area where the pace of innovation is rapid, this can be a real problem for suppliers:

> There's not usually disagreement about the fact something is wanted. It's a question of the degree to which it is wanted, or by how many. There is a bit of a tendency, I think, because it is a fast-moving area, to listen to the last input. You know, because somebody has spoken to a customer, who looks like a pretty big customer, this person who seems to be in an influential position said they want this or they won't buy, then we have a tendency to say, we must do this just to make sure of the business. But it's difficult to say how right or wrong that is. On the one hand you want to be responsive to what customers say, on the other hand you can't be changing direction every five minutes, otherwise you never complete anything.
>
> *Do you think that's an occupational hazard for people who work in close contact with end-users, that they tend not to be able to compile a strategic vision of the marketplace?*
>
> Well, you could call it an occupational hazard but you could also say it was being responsive to customers. It's difficult to know where the line goes.
> (Section head, R&D, Telewave Electronics)

Equally, what customers want may often be difficult for R&D engineers to anticipate or accept, because they rest on non-technical needs.

> It's very easy to sit in here and rationalise away about why a customer doesn't need something, and we're all very good at it. You can say, the customer is asking for a particular feature, a real-time decoder – never mind what that means – and we've said to them, do you really want real-time decode? The information comes up too fast to read; surely that's

no use to you? Why don't you capture the data and look at it later? They say, yes, you're right, but I still like it because it gives me a warm feeling that I'm capturing the data I want, I don't read it all as it comes past but it's still useful. We would have said, oh well, that's not all that useful to him and put it off, put it down our priority list. So it goes on and on and on. At the end of the day you've got to give in to that. You can't logically see why somebody wants something, but you have to accept it.

(Product marketing engineer, Telewave Electronics)

If you intend to be truly responsive to the market, you have to accept that it is not as rational an animal as it appears in economic theory. Computing equipment is purchased and operated by human beings, prone to human failings such as wanting to see data even when it is scrolling too quickly to be read: cost–benefit analysis is not the only factor at work in purchasing decisions. This kind of information about what users want is unpredictable: it has nothing to do with engineering logic, but it is very real none the less. Unless your feedback loops are able to capture this kind of idiosyncratic, almost ethnographic information about user attitudes, as well as the more prosaic technical issues, your vision of the market will always be incomplete. If you are serious about incorporating user experience into the development, marketing and sale of your products, the first step has to be to understand how experience is transmitted between users and suppliers. You need to know the networks involved, what kinds of information flow along them, and where these networks lead into your organisation. Only then will you be able to think constructively about how to facilitate the processes involved, and turn the rhetoric of market responsiveness into a genuine sensitivity to user needs.

GATHERING FEEDBACK 1: INFORMAL LOOPS

When technical experts in suppliers are asked about how they know about user needs, in what contexts they come into contact with personnel from customer companies, and where their knowledge of user experience of products comes from, something quite interesting happens. Invariably, they refer first of all to formal mechanisms linking the supplier to the marketplace, which usually lead through sales and marketing departments before arriving in the R&D laboratory: a detailed consideration of these mechanisms is the subject of the next section of this chapter. They mention the different forms of market intelligence gathered by marketing departments, the monitoring of technical problems reported by maintenance engineers, the analysis of sales figures, and talking to salespeople about user opinion. Sometimes they mention a particular sub-division of marketing or sales which has a specific brief to encourage contacts between users and suppliers, and they dutifully attend the occasional customer visit or user group meeting. Their favourite way of keeping abreast of the competition is to get hold of a piece of competitor equipment and pull it to pieces, carrying out a full technical assessment.

However, when pressed further about user feedback, it becomes clear that these organisational structures are overlaid by cross-cutting networks of personal contacts, friendships and professional peer relationships. These play as important a role in bringing people from suppliers and customers into direct contact as formalised organisational links. They are frequently more effective as a way of transmitting information precisely because they are non-institutional: the members of the network are free to pass on information they consider relevant, rather than have relevance defined for them. This lack of an externally imposed framework means that informal networks are extremely flexible, capable of carrying a range of detail that stretches from highly technical information to personal gossip – both of which might be equally important to understanding how a user operates or how equipment performs.

Informal feedback loops are of three basic types. First there are professional loops, the networks created by the professionalisation of expertise. Their most visible manifestations are professional and trade associations, such as the Institute of Electronic and Electrical Engineers and the Institute of Managers, which provide forums for managers and experts from both users and suppliers to meet 'on neutral ground', exchange opinions and debate technical issues. For all the participants, the chance to build up their network of professional contacts is one of the explicit motives given for attending. Trade fairs and exhibitions form part of the professional loop as well, and trade magazines allow specialists to keep in touch with technical and business developments in their field. The higher you go in an organisation, the more likely it becomes that the people in senior positions will already know their opposite numbers in other companies through a professional loop. In a technically specialised area a professional network is frequently used as a recruitment channel, with companies acquiring expertise in particular areas by poaching talent from a user or supplier on the basis of a recommendation by a professional peer.

Professional loops, by their nature, are excellent transmitters of technical information: they assume a shared technical expertise and vocabulary, and the diffusion of technical knowledge is one of the explicit objectives of trade associations and magazines. In the context of product development cycles, for example, they are important as the basis of engineer–engineer dialogue, or what some R&D engineers call 'the next-bench syndrome'. Designers of a specialised piece of equipment are often in a position where they have a professional colleague who either is or could be an end-user, inside or outside their company; 'market research' therefore often consists of getting in touch with a peer and finding out what features they would like in a new product or their assessment of the strengths and weaknesses of an existing product. But technical information is not the only material transmitted by professional loops. They are also a forum for the circulating of insider information about company fortunes, personnel movements and job terms and conditions, often in the form of extremely informal – even scurrilous – rumour and gossip. This information is important to professionals, who are often very mobile, circulating regularly between a limited number of companies and preoccupied with negotiating terms as they move, and they need to be able to tap into a shared pool of knowledge which is assumed to provide 'the real picture' rather than the idealised image companies present to outsiders. Inevitably, the more professional loops deal in this kind of informal, privileged information, the more likely it becomes that some professional contacts blossom into genuine friendships, and become the starting point for the most informal, least structured kind of feedback loop, friendship networks.

The social networks of people working in the business world have received very little attention from researchers, but they often play a crucial role in business transactions because they are a convenient way of bypassing formal channels. The insider, non-documentary information they are best fitted to transmit is often so privileged that it could even be illegal, as in the case of insider trading. More usually, networks of friends are a framework through which customer needs can be channelled into a supplier in an unusually raw, uncensored form:

> I have friends in various parts of various customer organisations who would give one a lot of information, more than they should. *Are these people you have known for years?* In some cases, yes. I have a particular friend in Acme Electronics who used to work in Venus Telecommunications whom I knew at International Radar fifteen years ago. It's not quite bribery and corruption, but certainly personal contacts. People who for various reasons would like to see you get a job rather than another company. . . . For example, we got a job recently with one of those regional companies where they went out to tender to thirteen companies and knew perfectly well they wanted us, so there was a bit of bookcooking, well not quite, but finding ways of making sure the whole thing was presented to the Board to be signed in a way that favoured us.
> (Marketing manager, Defence Electronics)

Finally, there are commercial networks. These refer to the way technical information is transferred during the course of a commercial transaction.

Contrary to what might be expected, the actual outcome of the transaction, and even whether it is completed or not, tends not to affect the transmission of information between user and supplier. Part of a technical expert's working life will be spent responding to documents produced by users: tendering documents, for example, often include a great deal of technical material. Technical specialists from different companies will meet in a large number of commercial contexts: when visiting potential customers, or carrying out routine maintenance work, holding a plant open day, or user group meeting, preparing a tender bid, or thrashing out specifications with a components supplier, to name some obvious examples. Over time, these interactions between users and suppliers are a means through which technical feedback can be gathered, and new areas of expertise developed. This exploitation of existing commercial loops, rather than reliance on market research as traditionally defined, is how those who develop products both promote their expertise and build up their own ideas of what the market wants, together with the professional loops and friendship networks described above. All three of these feedback loops are pulled together in the following description of product development in Defence Electronics, by a marketing manager who was also a technical expert:

> As far as designing equipment is concerned, then the guys doing that read textbooks and they also go to conferences from time to time. They do some original thinking. They talk to components suppliers. Now, a components supplier will for example be a specialist company in amplifiers, or in frequency synthesiser circuits, so the system designer then, from the lower level to the hierarchy, will pick up information about the way companies are doing things, or how many things they can do on a single chip, or whatever. He may devolve that into his design. So it is very multifaceted.

In practice, then, much of the information that arrives in R&D laboratories about customers and their needs does not come via the formal structures – sales and marketing departments – that have been viewed as conduits of user experience, linking R&D departments to the marketplace. Obviously, the way informal feedback loops operate varies greatly according to the technology, branch of expertise and economic sector they are part of. For example, all the informal loops described above depend to some extent upon the nature of the user–supplier relationship. Friendship networks and professional loops in particular depend upon peers being in contact with each other for long enough to be able to develop a stable social relationship. This in turn is linked to the pace of innovation: in areas such as business computing, where innovation is very rapid and the market is segmenting, manyprofessional peers either fall off the pace of innovation or move into new niche specialisations that open up, which fragments old feedback loops even as it creates new ones. Equally, the long-term, stable user–supplier relationship that provides the most fertile soil for the growth of feedback loops is not as common as it was. Nevertheless, the fact remains that the managing director of a supplier genuinely concerned with incorporating user experience into product innovation ought to think along non-institutionalised lines.

The fact that much of the information that is transmitted between users and suppliers is carried by informal loops, which are effective and wide-ranging precisely because those in the loop are left to decide for themselves what information to circulate, means that it is by definition impossible to institutionalise an informal feedback loop through some organisational device. The essence of this kind of feedback is that it is informal, that it is not structured or constrained by forces external to the loop. In dealing with informal loops, senior management can only enable, not prescribe.

The first step is to ensure that senior management understand the importance and potential usefulness of informal loops: this is not difficult to demonstrate, given that professional loops and friendship networks play an especially important part in the working lives of senior managers. Once senior management has grasped the importance of informal loops through the critical examination of their own working routines, a company can begin to turn the rhetoric of responsiveness to users into reality. Staff should be encouraged to participate in professional associations and be sent to trade fairs and exhibitions, and any forum where personnel come into contact with customers and build up relationships with them should be actively patronised. Such forums include specialist courses, industry bodies, standardisation committees, training boards, professional associations and trade unions. There should be a company policy to involve as many R&D staff as possible in the response to documents produced by users, and a conscious nurturing of links with third parties: not just users, although they obviously have priority, but also suppliers, contractors and consultants. Finally, the cultivation of informal feedback loops should not be seen in isolation from the formal organisational loops every company has for gathering market intelligence and user reaction to products: formal and informal feedback loops are complementary, not mutually exclusive. Although they transmit different types of information, and encode user experience in different ways, suppliers need both if they are to compile a three-dimensional picture of the marketplace and the dynamics of change within it. It is not difficult to see why: while the market is overlaid by personal and professional networks, those in the networks are also, for the most part, members of organisations. They are individuals with social networks of their own, but these networks are partly intertwined with the formal structures through which many individuals in the marketplace meet. These should now be examined more closely.

GATHERING FEEDBACK 2: FORMAL LOOPS

All serious suppliers devote considerable time and effort to gathering feedback from the marketplace as systematically as possible, via formal mechanisms. Sales staff write reports on successful sales and post-mortems on failures, marketing staff survey actual and potential users, and maintenance engineers report on the technical performance of equipment. Sales and marketing departments have traditionally been the interface where supplier and customer first come into contact. Even in an outwardly collaborative relationship where senior management in both companies take each other golfing, it is still more likely to be the sales staff who will have most contact with customers and their needs. When senior managers return from their golfing weekends, however, the crucial management question from the viewpoint of the supplier is not so much who gathers the feedback as where it goes. You cannot give the market what it wants unless user experiences are incorporated into product development, embedded in the process of innovation itself. This means ensuring not just that feedback is gathered, but that it is transmitted to the managers and experts involved in product development.

In practice, this means that one of the most important priorities of the managing director must be to design the relationship between R&D and the rest of the company in such a way that customer feedback flows into product development as freely as possible. In other words, you need to look very closely at the organisational relationship between sales, marketing and R&D functions. Someone has to set the parameters within which R&D work takes place, which means accommodating the often conflicting claims of development engineers, and their judgements of what is technically possible, and those who say they know what the market wants, most of whom are not directly involved with product development. While they may not have as much technical knowledge as R&D people, they can use the greater amount of time they spend in the field as a device to give their opinions legitimacy and weight.

Difficult though this balancing act is, there is at least the example of how competitors have tried to deal with the problem. Before drawing some general conclusions on formal feedback loops and ways they can lead into R&D and product development cycles, we can get a flavour of real-world business problems by looking at how three particular suppliers grappled with the issue.

DEFENCE ELECTRONICS

Defence Electronics (DE) is a medium-sized British company, which produces a variety of civil and military products but depends mainly upon defence contracts. It has considerable experience in the research and development of radar, signalling and military electronics products, but despite its modern, high-technology product line DE is in many ways an archetypal British company, reproducing many of the class divisions of British society in its hierarchical, rather rigid company structure. It is emphatically not the kind of flexible, adaptable company Burns and Stalker would have called organic. In recent years it has attempted to expand beyond its core markets by acquiring overseas interests, but its experience of diversification was disastrous and lost the company a great deal of money. This in turn forced very significant job losses at some of its plants, and the hiving off of parts of its defence business to competitors. Although DE will survive, it seems fair to say that it is in the process of becoming a shadow of its former self, albeit for reasons which have nothing to do with its core product development cycles.

DE is divided into eight operating divisions, each working in a distinct technological area and responsible for its own design, development, project management, manufacturing, sales and marketing, reporting to a main board. Each operating division is sub-divided into a number of trading groups, organised around parts of the product range, each of which has its own sales, marketing and product development staff. At the end of the 1980s DE had a total of 24,000 employees and annual sales worldwide of over US$1.5 billion. A high proportion of employees, including sales and marketing personnel have scientific and professional qualifications. The company has traditionally been R&D driven, stressing research excellence as a basis for the steady rate of technical innovation that underpins its product line.

Sales and marketing staff are recruited internally in the first instance, and one of the problems which an emphasis on scientific excellence has generated is a certain difficulty in persuading technical experts to move out of R&D. It is also reflected in a perception of selling, especially, as a rather dubious activity for a 'techie', and managers were forced to stress the technically challenging nature of the work in order to attract and keep internal recruits:

> Two younger guys . . . migrated from development into sales because we recognised we needed more help on that and they were ready to get some more commercial experience. They were reluctant I would say in both cases, initially, because salesmen have a bad reputation, but I think they quickly realised that the sales side was still very technical, and therefore they satisfied that side of their ambitions.

In headcount terms, R&D departments in trading groups are many orders of magnitude greater than both sales and marketing: in the operating division where interviewing was carried out, the typical size of a sales team attached to a trading group was four, with marketing consisting of only one or two. Tellingly, DE conflated sales and marketing functions, with marketing activity carried out by both sales and marketing managers. Marketing activity, however, was defined in terms which would horrify many marketing specialists: it consisted largely of publicity work, with none of the systematic gathering of intelligence which makes up the work of marketing groups elsewhere. Formal feedback loops were difficult to find at DE: even the organisational mechanisms in place to gather user responses were honoured more in the breach than the observance:

> The quality manager keeps a record of returned items, for example, so you know what your fault rate is like. We don't always do that. What tends to happen, for example, the job with Acme, we're on our fifth contract, and whilst our project guy's there he gets told, by the way, we had a couple of faults on the contract of five years ago the other day, and we are a bit worried about the oscillators because they are dropping out once a month nowadays. Maybe we ought to do some refurbishing. That kind of thing. It's not very formal. Generally, trying to formalise things doesn't seem to work too well.

Other formal feedback mechanisms DE operates include recording and monitoring enquiries and setting up user groups, but the overall impression given was that informal feedback was relied upon far more for information about customers, and to construct ideas of what users wanted. It is not difficult to see why: DE's history as a defence contractor, with extremely stable, long-term relationships with its customers in the defence establishment, has allowed it to build up comprehensive professional and friendship networks to bind itself to its core clients in the military. DE's relationships with some clients stretch back for decades, and its history as a military supplier still conditions its approach to civilian business. The reason the salesforce is numerically small, technically expert and plays such a marginal role in setting company priorities, especially in product development, is that DE relies on established, long-term customers rather than touting for new business. The salesforce manages existing accounts, and the DE strategy is to ensure that salespeople have enough technical expertise to enter into specialist discussion. The company's business philosophy, together with a suspicion of any generalising approach which seemed to get in the way of niche supplying, was perfectly summed up by a middle-level marketing manager:

There is an overall worldwide DE international marketing activity, and there is a bunch of guys called the International Marketing Group who go galloping all round the world doing nobody any good and wasting a lot of the company's money. There's a lot of fighting going on at board level at the moment of how we run that kind of activity, whether it's any use to us. . . . As far as I am concerned, the real business is done the way we do it here, long-term close contact with customers with a strong technical bias, where you are looking for very very clearly defined strategic and practical advantages. . . . You need a guy who has a very deep understanding of the competitor advantages, and he needs to be steeped in that technology [to sell it].

DE's company history, its business philosophy and technical expertise were all therefore ideal for the kind of intense, engineer-to-engineer dialogue between DE and its users which, outside a defence contractor, might be taken as an excellent example of the user–supplier relationship. The balance of knowledge between DE and military users was fairly equal, with a critical mass of relevant experts on both sides able to conduct a detailed technical dialogue. User needs and experiences were genuinely incorporated into both formal and informal feedback loops. On the other hand, before presenting DE as a model supplier, it is worth remembering that outside the defence industry it is inconceivable that DE would have been able to build up the relationships it did, and that it would not survive for long were it forced to depend on non-defence business and expose itself to the kind of cold competitive winds that blow outside the peculiar world of the British defence industry.

DE, in short, has been lucky. As a reasonably large company, by British standards, producing high-technology military products, it has considerable strategic importance for the Ministry of Defence, anxious to source in Britain when possible. Its preference for stable, long-term user relationships, conditioned by its background in defence procurement, is reflected in an organisational structure that is markedly mechanistic, in terms of Burns and Stalker's typology: hierarchical, highly segmented and organisationally stable over time. However, many of its user relationships were only made possible by the absence of the kind of competitive pressures normal in the civil sector. Although DE does considerable civilian business, most of its civilian products depend on technologies spinning off from military work, such as signalling, radar and certain kinds of instrumentation. The level of competition it faces in these high-tech but very specialised markets has increased in recent years, but is still relatively low. This absence of competitive pressures has left DE vulnerable now that external factors have altered the commercial playing field. With the end of the Cold War its core defence business is in decline, and business pressures were racked up several notches by its ill-considered foreign acquisition. DE is now forced to restructure itself but is poorly equipped to do so: its staff is highly specialised, there is no company history of rapid organisational change, and redundancies have demoralised staff morale. It needs to find new markets to survive, but has the kind of specialist sales and marketing force which will find it extremely difficult to do this.

TELEWAVE ELECTRONICS

Telewave Electronics (TE) is a US-owned multinational corporation with a number of factories and sales divisions in Europe. It describes itself as designing, manufacturing and servicing electronic products and systems for measurement and computation. It ranks in the top 50 of the US *Fortune 500*, with sales of approximately US$9,900 million and profits of approximately US$820 million in 1990. It has 87,000 employees worldwide. In Britain TE has 4,000 employees, sales of approximately £500 million per annum, two manufacturing sites, four R&D sites and twenty-two sales/support offices. The sales office studied by us has sales of approximately £25 million per annum. It is the epitome of the expertise-based company. As unskilled and semi-skilled direct labour has shrunk to a tiny proportion of total costs, recent (albeit limited) growth in employment has been concentrated in sales, marketing and R&D. Never a company with a mass market image, it has increasingly concentrated on high-value products, with labour costs heavily weighted towards graduate engineering professionals. Known internationally as an 'engineering company', it has recently sought to strengthen its sales and marketing activity in an attempt to overcome the market's perception of it as having quality products which are hard to find out about and relatively expensive! Increasingly customers were perceived to be looking to competitors for a more basic, functional and cheaper product.

In the early 1980s TE redesigned its computer product line around RISC (reduced instruction set computing: simplicity in processing hardware against complexity in software). The first machine was shipped in late 1986, provoking near crisis when it looked as if the technology had failed. But 1988 saw the volume of sales grow by approximately 20 per cent. In test and measurement systems, software products are increasingly important and it is trying to define and break into new product markets, such as those concerned with intelligent telephone networks. What used to be distinct products and markets are converging around UNIX-based computing systems. TE has typically been regarded as a market leader in instrumentation, though facing increasing competition from Japan, and as a challenger in the computer systems sector. Unlike many other international suppliers, TE seems to be weathering a long economic recession relatively well, continuing in profit and moving upwards in the Datamation 'Top Ten'.

TE is a supplier of test and measurement systems to DE, but in terms of its business philosophy and organisation structure it could not be more different. In Burns and Stalker's terms, it is a good example of the organic system. When recruitment was more active, there was a one-way migration of engineering labour from DE to TE, not just because of TE's favourable pay rates but because it was widely perceived to be an interesting, challenging place to work, with a more humane management system. The corporation is well known for its progressive management, which is underpinned by a US- style corporate philosophy known as the TE Way. The philosophy is based on a carefully elaborated, human resources approach to the management of the workforce. It is committed to growth through continuous innovation, with profit as its primary objective. The expertise of people at all levels is regarded as the key resource through which innovation is maintained. The goal of maximising profit through continuous innovation is regarded as compatible with the goal of maximising individual growth and the fulfilment of individual potential. The corporate ideology seeks to establish the groundwork for shared values and ideals and to emphasise a unity of purpose amongst all levels of the workforce and all social categories:

> We believe our diverse workforce helps TE realise its full potential. Recognising and developing the talents of each individual brings new ideas to TE. The company also benefits from the innovation that results when TE people work together who have differing experiences and perspectives. In this way, a well-managed diverse workforce expands our base of knowledge, skills and understanding. It also enables us to be more responsive to the needs of our customers.
>
> In order to reap these benefits, we need extra attention and commitment from every individual. Managers, in particular, play a critical role and are responsible for creating a work environment in which the contributions of all people can be recognised. To do this they need to understand how best to utilise individual talents so that people's special attributes can be used to achieve company objectives. Managers must also communicate this attitude to our people who should reflect it in working with fellow employees, customers, vendors and the general public.
>
> TE needs to continue to identify and attract a workforce of the best talent available in each location where we operate. Our ability to use our diversity to realise our full potential will be an important factor in achieving future success in the global marketplace.
>
> (TE corporate promotional literature)

The corporate philosophy is reinforced materially by single status terms and conditions of employment, above average pay rates, share ownership, private health care schemes, and a high level of other social benefits inside and outside work. The majority of the workforce has security of employment, but not job security: people are expected to be flexible and to accept job transfers according to requirements defined by periodic restructuring. TE has always been a non-union employer. The belief is that the management style, performance appraisal procedures, training provision and level of remuneration obviate the need for trade unions.

TE has a sophisticated human resources model of the employment contract which emphasises the individualistic character of the relationship between the company and the employee. Pay is negotiated annually between each individual and his or her manager, on the basis of the performance review. Managers claim to make themselves available and accessible at all times to discuss, and diffuse, grievances quickly. Security of employment and a developed internal labour market sustain the belief that opportunities for improved pay and status are dependent not on collective action but solely on the individual's motivation, ability and achievement. The ideology is strictly meritocratic: in theory anyone can get to the top, if they show themselves willing and able and have the drive to complete appropriate training.

Labour turnover at TE is very low and company loyalty is high. This is reinforced not only through a high level of material benefits and responsive, accessible management, but also through the internal labour market. Once selected, individuals will generally be redeployed, with retraining and counselling if necessary, if their existing job disappears, or if they do not meet the performance requirements of the job. At higher levels, it is unusual for managers to be appointed from outside TE, although geographical mobility is frequently necessary to attain promotion. TE also discourages poaching of its engineers, through a commitment to continuous development, as well as high levels of remuneration. The main forum for discussion of career moves is the annual performance review, carried out by each employee's supervisor or manager. It is emphasised, however, that it is up to the individual to take the initiative in identifying a career path and to set agreed performance objectives along this path with their manager. Subsequent rewards will be tied to the attainment of these objectives. Overall the belief is that security of employment, training and promotion opportunities and good financial benefits will generate good employment relations and the conditions necessary for continuous technical innovation.

In return the company expects high levels of commitment, effort and continuous improvements in performance. No one is expected to come to work simply to pass the time and there is considerable peer group pressure on individuals to fall into line or move on. Thus any problems are firmly located with the individual, not the company, and counselling will be directed to this effect. By implication individuals carry the blame for their own relative failure and, since there is in reality a very small number of promoted posts, most people will be relative failures. It is typically those in middle management who experience the contradictions between the espoused ideals and the reality of restricted career mobility most strongly, particularly when recession means little or no growth in jobs and little movement up the ladder. In general, however, pay and benefits are relatively high, many people have intrinsically interesting jobs and there is a high degree of acceptance of the TE Way: 'the opportunities are there, it's up to the individual to take them' is an often-heard comment.

The main carriers of the TE Way are the managers and supervisors who are trained in communication skills and are expected to be accessible and approachable at all times. This is facilitated by open plan factory design, with integrated production and office areas; senior managers are routinely visible to their staff, and cafeteria and coffee areas are shared. Status differences between levels are minimised by the use of first names and by the deliberate informality of a dress code in which shirt sleeves dominate and those reluctant to take their jackets off are likely to be seen as stand-offish. The company emphasises the value of 'management by wandering around' as a means of keeping in touch with feeling at the grass roots. The aim is to create an ethos whereby any individual can approach his or her manager or others to discuss a problem, or proceed to the next level manager if no resolution is forthcoming.

A major plank in the production arrangements which seek to ensure high-quality goods and continuous improvement in manufacturing processes is the use of just-in-time (JIT) and total quality management (TQM) techniques. JIT is a minimum inventory production system which aims to build products to order rather than for stock, to cut work in progress and to reduce product completion times. TQM aims to make everyone responsible for the quality of the finished goods, at each stage from development to production, and to improve the links between product design, marketing and manufacturing. The use of JIT production has been accompanied by increased use of subcontracting of work previously done in-house. TE is concentrating increasingly on high-tech electronics and buys in mechanical and electro-mechanical sub-assemblies from contractors.

Product development in the customer-responsive firm

TE is a particularly good example of the contemporary move to make product development more responsive to customers. Over a period of ten years, corporate management has sought to redirect the structure away from an R&D emphasis towards marketing. In the face of competition from the Far East, the objective has been to make the business look outward to the market rather than inward toward the laboratory. The official line is that its concern has shifted from the design of products solely for technical innovation towards getting products out to the market faster and equipped to meet customer requirements including price. Hence pressure has been put on divisions to shorten development timetables in order to create the desired responsiveness to the customer. The language of TQM and talk about both internal and external customers has been used to persuade laboratory engineers to work collaboratively, and on an equal footing, with marketing and manufacturing.

The customer-responsive ideology is explicit in much company literature:

TE's basic business purpose is to provide the capabilities and support needed to help customers worldwide improve their personal and business effectiveness.

(Annual report, 1988)

All over the UK Companies like [Domestic Goods Inc.] are choosing TE as their Partner in design systems. . . . They find that we offer the problem-solving you'd expect from a good consultant together with the systems knowhow of a leading manufacturer. It's a unique approach.

(Advertising copy, 1989)

The emphasis is on partnership with our customers, helping them and they helping us, by sharing common ideas and what each does best.

(Partners in productivity seminars, 21 May 1989)

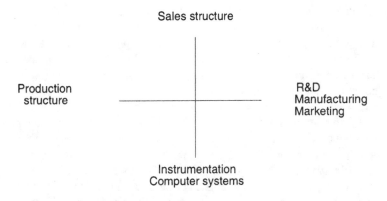

Figure 1 The division of expert labour at the interface of sales, marketing and R&D in Telewave Electronics

As part of our research we explored the product development process in one division of TE and tried to assess the effectiveness of the customer-responsive ideology for product development. We explore below the extent to which there is genuine collaboration between R&D, marketing and manufacturing and assess the quality of customer involvement. TE is a matrix organisation (see Figure 1) with a structure designed to distinguish between the sales generalists, who are meant to present the united front of TE to the customer, and the production specialists with responsibility for getting products onto the market. The production structure relates to a particular product line, while the sales structure relates to a geographical region. Thus sales representatives in Britain may be selling systems manufactured in Germany or the USA, while sales representatives in California may be selling systems manufactured in Europe. Within the production structure is a marketing function concerned with product applications; this is staffed by engineers many of whom move there from R&D.

Although the matrix structure is relatively enduring, the detailed allocation of responsibilities between, for example, product marketing and sales is continually under negotiation. Members of the firm are proud of their ability to negotiate perpetually changing remits, responsibilities and relationships: 'you'll find there are dotted lines all over, a myriad of them. We're a hell of a complex company. The beauty of it is that everyone knows everybody else by first name. . . . Change is the one constant' (district sales manager). Conventionally TE has been R&D led; the sales organisation has regarded the divisions as too slow to bring products to market and as insufficiently attuned to what sells, as opposed to what is technically possible in the absence of time or budget constraints.

The organic structure and rhetoric of common goals had not, over a period of forty years or so, prevented divisions from identifying more with local than with corporate success, or from seeking bigger empires at home. Traditionally each TE division had its own technical specialism, and was solely responsible for developing, marketing and manufacturing products in that range. This had led to competition between divisions who found that they were selling overlapping products to the same customers, with sales staff acting at cross purposes. Corporate management had begun to regard the autonomy of divisions as damaging their ability to compete with other suppliers, particularly in market areas where component products were increasingly being combined into systems. They lacked the capacity to pool common expertise, located in different divisions, in order to win contracts. Corporate management began to argue that the duplication of R&D and manufacturing facilities, in overlapping technical spheres, was unjustifiably expensive. They appeared to be losing out both in terms of the ability to put together new combinations of expertise to win systems contracts and in terms of the ability to produce a basic, lower cost product to counter new competition in their traditional markets.

Corporate strategy therefore sought to introduce a greater degree of centralised control over product development, marketing and manufacturing. Structurally, performance measurement systems were changed to reflect performance of the product group in international, instead of domestic markets and the senior management reward system was tied to international product line success, not the success of the local facility. For the first time in the latter part of the 1980s, a clear-cut division was made between the location of R&D and that of manufacture, with the aim of gradually centralising and concentrating R&D expertise, while siting manufacturing plants strategically for access to targeted markets. As far as corporate management was concerned, such centralised redirection was compatible with a broadly organic philosophy. Although the process of redirection was not without its setbacks and reversals, and is far from complete, on the whole the organic structure and ideology seemed to have facilitated the reorientation of division managers away from local arenas towards viewing themselves as competing in a global market (Webb and Dawson, 1991).

At division level this reorientation to world markets had to be operationalised and translated into changes in the day-to-day management of development, marketing and manufacturing. At the time of our study, the main vehicle signifying the change was the business team, comprising middle managers and engineers from marketing, R&D and manufacturing for each product group. In part this was meant to provide a channel for insights from less senior staff into the development cycle and to prevent the domination of business practice by senior management. It was also meant to facilitate continuing discussion about the qualities of new product proposals in terms of their likely market potential and ease of manufacture. Formally at least R&D was no longer completely autonomous, but had to be accountable to marketing and manufacturing. Although the business team was seen by middle management as having limited value in preventing the domination of strategy by senior management, there was an explicit commitment to the notion of a triad of R&D, marketing and manufacturing. Meanwhile, formal stages in the development process were evolving in such a way that systematic input from marketing and manufacturing were becoming routine. The formal mechanisms consisted of a series of stages imposed on an annual cycle, from the investigation of ideas, involving R&D and marketing; the definition of a product (a generic set of features emerging out of discussions with customers); assessment of costs, timescales and production technology; design of prototypes to be tried out on key customers; assessment of market viability; and finally production.

Marketing sought increasingly to veto products with little or no sales potential at an early stage. Each stage included formal signing-off meetings, although in practice recycling through some stages was not uncommon, particularly in new product areas. Customer input was regarded as vital throughout, but there was a distinction between generation and selection of new *features*, which was perceived as marketing's territory, and product *breakthroughs*. The latter were seen as the key to market power but were felt to be increasingly difficult to realise, because of intense competition to get state of the art products out the door. For new product markets, the formal stages were underpinned by a high level of informal exchange, as engineers sought to define a product with potential customers:

> our customers are convinced that they've got to be able to analyse what's going on between these two computers controlling a network, but what exactly they're going to be looking for they're not so sure. So our definition for this product is a lot more flexible.
>
> (Product manager, marketing)

Most conflict between the perspectives and roles of marketing and R&D seemed to occur when the division of labour between them was at its least formal, the investigation phase of development. R&D continued to prioritise technical advance while marketing tried to argue for what would sell, according to their investigation of customer requirements:

> The inevitable attraction for people in R&D is to go at the second generation product. However business-wise that doesn't always make the best sense; the best sense is that the earlier you get your money the more valuable it is. . . . And if you're not successful with this product here, the second generation product is not worth doing. . . .
>
> (Product manager, marketing)

> Once we've decided what we're going to do . . . and you've got a reasonable idea of what the price is going to be . . . and all the rest of it, the roles are better defined. Product marketing will get on and write its data sheets and competitive analyses. . . . And R&D would go ahead and design things the way they thought they ought to be designed.
>
> (Product manager, marketing)

Informally at least there still appeared to be a status hierarchy in place, with R&D at the top. High flying electronics graduates began in R&D, with exits to marketing and manufacturing engineering. The ideal R&D engineer was meant to be both highly trained and youthful: 'it's a young man's [sic] game' (R&D manager). Most importantly they needed the intangible and mysterious quality of vision: 'that guy has got to have vision for his products' and 'fire in his belly' (R&D manager), a quality which we were told above all distinguishes the laboratory engineer from others. With the vision they 'lead R&D effort and product strategy into a segment of our target market' (R&D manager). It took two to three years to find out whether someone recruited to the laboratory had this quality; if not they would move on: 'some [R&D engineers] are just interested in the technical aspects of it. And some people are more interested in what happens to the things they work on afterwards, that is who buys it, who uses it, is it successful and so on' (product manager, marketing). The latter join marketing. The movement seemed to be entirely in this direction despite the fact that 'some people might claim it's more desirable the other way round!' (product manager, marketing). The laboratory engineers regarded themselves as the locus of technical creativity, working to professional standards set by the technological community rather than the marketplace. They had limited formal contact with customers; marketing engineers and the field sales staff were regarded as the direct link:

> When you start off, you're very close to making electrons do what you want them to do, and then to start interacting with the outside world, it's not easy. . . . I remember many instances of things that customers were asking for that I argued didn't make sense, what they were asking for was technically stupid . . . and was.
>
> (Ex-laboratory engineer)

The structural solution to making the 'visionary' more accountable to the paying customers has been to strengthen the marketing function, placing marketing managers as intermediaries between customers, sales and R&D. In contrast to the masculine depiction of R&D work, product marketing was described in stereotypical feminine terms, as dealing with feelings about a market share, rather than the 'hard facts' of the technology. The role of the marketing engineer seemed to be to persuade and influence rather than to assert technical direction. They needed to be able to decide when to push an idea and when to let it drop: 'I know there have been a number of times when we would modify products which the R&D manager didn't want us to do . . . we can't possibly act on everything that comes back in [from users] . . . so the product managers have to [identify] the best opportunity commercially and then try to persuade the lab that it makes technical and commercial sense' (marketing manager). Marketing managers provide the field news: 'typically marketing is much more *au fait* with . . . a real-time basis' (R&D manager). Information about the customer routinely came to the laboratory engineer in the form of 'strange ideas about daily sheets and things like that' (former laboratory engineer), which is a euphemism for saying that marketing deals in woolly concepts such as market share. To an outsider of course what sells seems a lot closer to hard facts than the movement of electrons, but the laboratory engineers had captured the high ground of scientific authority.

Although laboratory engineers viewed themselves as increasingly market driven, they did not regard themselves as marketing driven, which was described by the laboratory manager as resulting in a 'laundry list approach' to product design, producing feedback on product features rather than new insights. The orientation to customers via marketing was regarded as too vague to generate real innovation; the feedback coming via sales channels was too diverse, needed to be prioritised and commonly arrived too late for the laboratory engineers, who had already moved on to a new project. Strengthening the marketing function had resulted in more systematic feedback from customers on the desired features for product enhancements, but had not produced a convincing means of leading the market with innovatory design. The relative status hierarchy of the two functions was thus preserved, and R&D continued to believe that there was no textbook solution to the problem of customer-responsive innnovation.

It was the problem of 'how to get the right products at the right time' (R&D manager) which preoccupied the R&D group. Even in TE no one had any guaranteed solutions. This is not to suggest that R&D did not have a view on how to work towards the next technical breakthrough, and it was a view which relied on customers, but not through any formal structural links. The above description may have given the impression that product development took place in a social vacuum, broken only by field reports from marketing or sales. In fact technical innovation was a highly social activity, with key insights provided by regular, relatively informal contact with a cohort of other engineers, especially those employed by large customer firms. R&D engineers were chiefly responsive to a technological community of peers and continued to be centrally concerned with the technical excellence of the product. Like any artist with a vision, however, they regarded many paying customers as poor judges. It was technical peers in firms such as Defence Electronics (DE) whose views they respected. These were often engineers who worked in a development capacity, frequently using TE systems in the laboratory. Potential technical leads were derived by making extensive use of such user networks. A cohort of 'key guys' was used repeatedly over many years and added to periodically, depending on hot tips from field sales or news gleaned from conferences and meetings of standards bodies about 'who is really pushing the boat out' technically. Some users were latched onto for their vision about the direction of the business in a target area. Both marketing and R&D would expect continuing contact with such sources, though marketing saw itself as representing the external customer internally, and as having its own internal customer in the field sales staff.

Thus corporate-directed restructuring had had an effect on the management of product development, but the formal structure had not provided a convincing means of leading the market. Informal peer relationships remained the key to innovation, as far as the laboratory engineers were concerned. Customer feedback was a central resource, and had always been a factor in product development. It had become more consciously practised and more systematically elaborated through the structured involvement of marketing, but this had not resolved the real anxiety of R&D managers, which was how they continued to open up new technical directions. For the latter, it was a small community of powerful customers and their engineers who provided a source of inspiration and who carried real influence. Even in an organic system like that used by TE, the search for a customer-responsive organisation is far from over. Despite taking the initiative with customer engineers, and having a marketing group which understood the organisational politics of who to speak to and how to identify the 'user', they had not solved the problem of a rapid response to markets. Nor had the structure of TE guaranteed protection from the diverting effects of rivalries between specialisms, although these tensions appeared less destructive than in other firms. We should also remember that our study took place in the context of an R&D group under threat from corporate restructuring and the attempted centralisation of R&D effort in a few centres of excellence. This tacit agenda made the anxieties about the next technical breakthrough particularly acute and no doubt made the formal channels to the customer via marketing seem cumbersome and slow. The dilemma for senior management was that over-rigid control over development activity risked losing insights which might just be vital to innovation, while too much informality would result in an absence of any finished products. Senior managers thus struggled to control the deployment of technical expertise, while allowing sufficient autonomy of the middle ranks of engineers for new insights to develop.

Nevertheless, throughout the period of fieldwork, we never had the feeling that TE was anything other than a self-confident, reasonably successful company. It had faults, but it also engaged in searching self-analysis to try and pinpoint them. The key advantage of TE stemmed not from any specific formal innovation in organisation structure, but from the willingness of managers and engineers to experiment with different structures, without seeing such changes as a cause for a retreat into defensiveness. Tensions over who had the initiative for new developments were by no means resolved, but this was a source of negotiation between the functional groups, not a recipe for failure. However, as our next case study company showed, one firm's meat is another firm's poison. An attempt to institutionalise market responsiveness can have disastrous consequences. If it can save some companies, it can certainly prove the death of others.

MIDAS PLC

> There was an element right at the top of the company of 'we can't do anything wrong, everything we touch turns to gold, therefore we'll touch this and we'll touch that'.
>
> (Founder engineer)

At the beginning of our research, Midas plc was a medium-sized British company, of ten years' standing, struggling to regain a competitive position in the computer components industry. In 1990 it employed approximately 800 people, distributed between Britain, the USA and Singapore, developing and manufacturing high-tech, high-value disk drives. Since restructuring in 1989 most of its directors (retitled vice presidents) and its managing director had been based in the USA. It was a supplier to a subsidiary of TE and increasingly sought to emulate its organic management philosophy, including the appointment of an aspiring ex-TE engineer to the job of development manager.

Its founders were electrical and electronic engineers, who broke away from a US-owned multinational firm with an idea for a product which their employer had been reluctant to develop. The aim of the founders was to be at the leading edge of technical innovation, by being the first to introduce a microprocessor into the device. The company initially enjoyed tremendous success due, according to one of the founders, to the coincidence of timing: a newly emerging personal computer and workstation market and the availability of engineers with the required technical expertise. The first generation of products was widely perceived as highly innovatory and few competitors were able to produce an equally advanced device:

> Everybody wanted these disk drives and the ethos of our company always was to design one step ahead of everyone else. . . . In fact we weren't unique in Europe but we were the first guys in Europe with this type of product. . . . So that also heightened interest in the company because our major competitors were all Californian.
>
> (Founder engineer)

Midas was regarded as remarkable and held up as an example to other European companies because of its apparent success in 'beating the North Americans'. This success depended on close and continuing contact with prospective customers. In an open, expanding market, having a technological lead was a powerful means to shape and define customer requirements. Being responsive was largely a matter of informal alliances and contacts: suppliers were actively sought out by willing customers. In the most literal sense, the founders knew what would sell to computer manufacturers, because they broke away from a multinational which itself was a potential customer. It was from the multinational company that they recruited the skilled engineers who developed the first products and through their multinational company experience that they were able to create contacts in potential customers. User input into product development was direct, informal and technically creative for the engineers: 'during the same period [of initial design work] we were talking to potential customers and getting feedback from them and putting plans in place' (founder engineer). Midas was thus instrumental in shaping the emerging market and influencing customer perceptions of the qualities desirable in the product. They could operate flexibly, there was no historical 'baggage' and the market came to them. Revenues poured in; according to the vice president of engineering, price was no object and the company was making a 400 per cent profit over and above labour and materials costs.

The downside of such early success was that it contributed to a growing conviction amongst top management that they could do no wrong:

> I think Midas became a very arrogant company in terms of its dealings with all facets of industry – suppliers, customers, investors, bankers. . . . And I think we had a bad reputation for being too big for our boots.
>
> (Founder engineer)

By the latter part of the 1980s large profits had turned to large losses. By this time, the character of the market had changed and the balance of power had shifted in favour of customers. Other North American and Japanese suppliers had eroded Midas's technological lead and were able to sell the product more cheaply. Within Midas lack of attention to costs and the competition meant that, when the industry began to favour efficient practices, there were no routines for analysing management processes or identifying the profitable aspects of the business. Although the effects of the first high-tech recession were being felt throughout the electronics industry, Midas management continued to expand product lines and manufacturing facilities, apparently unable to identify the effect of their actions on profitability. According to a number of informants, a key aspect of the problem could be traced to the introduction of the first product incorporating a microprocessor, which also involved a technical leap to a higher capacity device. Outstanding design problems were left unresolved and production went ahead with low yields and a high failure rate amongst those products leaving the plant. They were making far too many products, including investing roughly US$25 million in the development of a high-capacity drive which was never manufactured: 'we were badly let down, mind you, by one company with whom we had contracted from the early days of the product, who in the end said we don't want it any more' (founder engineer). During the same period the founders opted to set up an expensive North American manufacturing facility and subsequently a retail division. The main motivation for creating such a plant in the USA, at a time when competitors were setting up automated facilities in Singapore or Thailand, was initially to supply Apple. Gaining this blue chip customer was regarded as a considerable accomplishment and depended once again on an informal and close liaison between customer and supplier:

> We got into them because they had an in-house disk group. They had developed a unique interface, but couldn't make it work. So they went out to every disk-drive company and said can you make a disk drive to this interface? Because Apple is Apple, everybody rushed to try and develop it and we happened to manage to succeed – and made 100,000 of them.
>
> (Principal engineer)

Such success in working collaboratively with new customers depended on appropriately skilled engineers. The former principal engineer, widely regarded as a technical genius, was described as the key person in the team who was able to fix the problems that customers had, not with Midas products, but with their own in-house systems:

> In the past, Apple had a problem . . . they just couldn't get the interface architecture . . . and Andrew went in there and spent several weeks fixing it. . . . So he has that kind of relationship with customers. He is well respected. That's a unique 'interface' the company has.
>
> (Senior engineer)

Ironically, Midas lost the supply contract when Apple demanded price reductions which Midas was unable to meet. Instead they set up in competition, entering the retail market with a packaged drive which could be plugged in to an Apple personal computer. Despite generating considerable revenues, the venture never proved profitable. Midas progressively lost its Original Equipment Manufacturer (OEM) customer base; its product range became uneconomic to manufacture; it lacked financial controls and failed to monitor, and react to, its own declining performance. Close relationships with customers became a thing of the past:

> We have had close contact with just about every major computer manufacturer in the world and over the time that Midas has been in existence we have probably lost just about all of them.
>
> (Principal engineer)

The 1988 results showed losses of US$25 million on revenues of US$120 million. Costs continued to increase while sales went into steep decline. Market share was bought by selling the products for less than the cost of the materials that went into them. Meeting the weekly payroll became a recurring nightmare. The legacy of financial systems designed for an expanding market and booming sales was the continuing accumulation of costly materials and a warehouse full of unsold goods. Layoffs followed and creditors ceased to be paid. In March 1989 the auditors' report effectively closed down operations. Such was the reserve of goodwill towards Midas that, following a joint management and bank coup, which forced the resignation of the founders, the company was refinanced with US$20 million in new money, supported chiefly by one of the clearing banks and 3i plc. The company was restructured with the appointment of a new chairman and financial director, both based in the USA.

Restructuring was accompanied by a new approach to business management, oriented to operating in a tighter market, with raised customer expectations. The firm had good technical resources and highly skilled engineers, as demonstrated by its past successes, albeit in the context of US competitors with significantly greater financial resources. The new senior management team set out to replace what was by now perceived as the inherited 'closed and arrogant' (vice president of engineering) approach to the business with an open collaborative style of management. Business plans were discussed with customers, suppliers and competitors, total quality management was advocated and systematic development of workforce expertise was sought through the appointment of a number of experienced managers to prominent roles in design, production and quality engineering. Formal structures were created to control product development timetables and to create a perceived missing communication link between the design team, manufacturing and customers. The espoused objective of senior management was to create an open, collaborative approach to the business, involving all relevant sources of expertise in the definition and implementation of business strategy. This organic style was meant to facilitate flexibility and innovation and was reflected in the flat organisation structure which consisted of a chairman and managing director with vice presidents of engineering, operations, quality, sales and marketing, human resources and finance. Each vice president was reported to by a manager and related support staff. The structure was relatively fluid, with changes continually taking place during the period of the study.

Product development and customer involvement: what went wrong with management strategy?

Only a small number of computer suppliers continue to design and manufacture disk drives in-house. The large OEMs have typically developed a subcontract relationship with at least two suppliers whose products are expected to be compatible. It is perceived as an intensive technical relationship which goes beyond the normal bounds of commercial dealings.

Because of the significance of the drive for the performance of the computer, customers have to understand the technology in detail. Some customers spend considerable time in the supplier's workplace, advising on technical aspects of the product and on production control. They are generally larger and better resourced than Midas.

Business strategy emphasised retrieving the OEM customer base through intensive liaison and renewed attempts to develop products which would out-perform the competition. The main structural solution created to ensure the renewal of contact with customers was the customer support organis-ation. This was headed by an ex-design engineer, who became chiefly responsible for customer feedback on products and for negotiating with customers the technical standards which they expected to be met by new developments. The customer support organisation was intended to protect the design team from constant interruption by customer demands and to act as a filter for information, such that design could respond not to the trivia but to key developments in the product market. In practice, the new language of 'partnership' meant that customers had to be actively courted, as they set higher standards of quality and reliability and sought to play suppliers off against each other. The group consequently had an expanding role, as a result of the articulation by major customers of vendor management policies: 'the larger OEMs want to know exactly what your production line deals are for that particular week on an ongoing basis' (customer support manager). The other formal structure for customer feedback was the marketing group, which sought to gather market intelligence on customer requirements and competitor products and to feed this in to the design process.

The objective was no longer to be a market leader, but to be 'just behind the bleeding edge' (development manager), or, in other words, to be engaged in a type of development described by the founder engineering director as the 'me too' product. Disk-drive technology remains in a state of continuous change, with new materials and techniques becoming available which are designed to increase the capacity, speed, reliability and accuracy of the device as well as making it more intelligent and decreasing relative costs. Miniaturisation has been dramatic, from washing machine size ten years ago to pocket size today. Many companies in the sector could not survive the intensity of competition, and miniaturisation of the product has been accompanied by concentration in the industry, from approximately forty companies to less than ten. Midas was the sole remaining European manufacturer of devices at the high capacity end of the range. But it had no history of success in designing and marketing 'me too' products. This depended on a different set of skills from those needed to leapfrog the competition, including attention to detail, precision in design, manufacturing and marketing, and an open dialogue with customers:

if you are plodding you have to make sure you plod absolutely accurately because there is no room to make mistakes, because you are bringing in a 'me too' product and if it is not designed absolutely impeccably, its yields, its margins and all its things will suffer and it's me too late and it's me too expensive and all the rest. . . . In the last two years I think people would argue we haven't really substantially brought out any new products. We are shipping a 200 megabyte drive and we were first with that one but if you actually look at it, we introduced it in November 1988 and it was in 1990 that we actually for the first time managed to get yields above 50 per cent. So it took us a long time to grind through a lot of the quality issues.

(Founder engineer)

Since the generation of significant revenue was dependent on winning supply contracts from the major computer manufacturers, the release of a prototype device in time for the annual trade fair, held every November in Las Vegas, was regarded as crucial. The perception of being in a race to market was in itself a source of constant anxiety, particularly when the company was low in confidence about its past commercial success and facing continuing uncertainty about its future.

No one was in any doubt about the value of the technical insights to be gained by working closely with customer engineers, but in practice the customer seemed to be becoming more, not less, remote from development:

Close relationships with customers are very important. They will tend to tell you what they expect and that will be based over the year from the competition. They won't reveal confidences but they will give enough clues to give you ideas as to what you should be aiming for. . . . Most of the successes we've had I think are where we get very heavily involved with the customer, where we not only just put in drives for evaluation but actually work with them to get them through the evaluation. Build up a personal . . . I think personal relationships have a lot to do with it. . . . If there is any problem and it's not resolved fairly quickly, you lose confidence. Doing it on the phone is always difficult. They talk to our customer people (in the region) who filter the information, who give it to our customer people over here who give it to us. It's nth handed by the time you get it and you don't believe it.

(Principal engineer)

Although the formal feedback networks had been set up with the intention of making customer input into design more efficient, in practice they appeared to be working to the detriment of the informal, peer and professional alliances which the engineers saw as central to technical innovation.

At an institutional level, the major customers had themselves changed. What the marketing manager described as 'the partnership bandwagon' meant that customers were trying to exert much greater leverage over their suppliers, in terms of functionality, quality and production scheduling. Both marketing and customer support managers spent significant periods of time negotiating with potential customers about the specification of new products and the potential for matching Midas development timetables with customer production schedules. This was a constant source of tension between marketing and development: marketing needed firm specifications and precise dates for prototypes, in order to be seen as credible by potential customers. Conversely it was in development's interests to retain as many degrees of freedom as possible. Being tied down to firm dates and specifications, which seemed unattainable in practice, was a recipe for antagonism between groups meant to be working together.

The language of partnership, moreover, was regarded as covering a variety of actual practices. Some customers were genuinely seen as constructive in their involvement. TE's subsidiary manufacturer of workstations, for example, was seen as keen to work with a supplier, including spending considerable time solving quality problems with the supplier's production engineering, an area of weakness for Midas:

> If they had a particular expertise or knew where to get it they would point us in the right direction. . . . Toing and froing really helps. . . . A lot of people were very sceptical, [but] there was give and take on both sides.
> (Midas design integrity engineer)

In this case the customer's expertise was used to develop process control measures and to analyse Midas business functions: highly intrusive, but in this case perceived as genuinely constructive. Midas unfortunately felt unable to exercise the same influence with its own suppliers, 'mainly because we don't have the same quality of vendor engineers' (design integrity engineer) – or perhaps the market clout.

Conversely other potential customers were perceived as expecting perfection first time and were impatient with those who failed to deliver it. Visits by engineers and marketing people to these firms were fraught: the firm's vendor engineers used the opportunity to insert new requirements into a tentative design specification, pushing up test costs for the supplier and testing out the supplier's willingness to promise to meet them. This was particularly prevalent as a negotiating tactic with Midas, because of its weak market position; customers could afford to be sceptical. In such a context, rebuilding reputation was crucial: another tension for design was thus created, between following through the minutiae of product integrity and getting a product out to customers for evaluation.

Ironically the 'me too' mentality meant that compatibility with competitors was a major issue: 'we end up doing changes to make ourselves more compatible with our competition' (principal engineer). Direct engineering contact with customers is focused on evaluation of the prototype drive for compatibility and performance, involving engineers in negotiation over technical standards. Tacitly, customers are communicating the promises made by other suppliers, but there is an area of doubt: who is bluffing whom? One obvious consequence for product development of this form of market responsiveness is that development is pulled in too many different directions by the 'wish lists' of customers, resulting in a lack of precision over defining products and priorities. Design changes would be introduced in development, some would be incorporated, some would be dropped, but most were not communicated to an aggrieved manufacturing group until late in the day.

Marketing exacerbated the tensions by continually alluding to 'being in the race', dragging the development group along by claims and rumours about what the competition was up to. Fluctuation and prevarication over design internally was further influenced by competitor announcements. In the attempt to shorten development timetables and find a quicker route to market, the formal specification kept changing. New technology was dropped or compromised: 'it all seems to be driven by the marketplace' (principal engineer). The main motivation in all this was matching the claims of the competition, often in the absence of hard data on actual products. Speculation replaced careful design and commitments to proceed were made before specifications were fully evaluated:

> The longer the thing slips, the more chance it has of changing, so the actual 400 meg we are working on just now is slipping. And the more it slips, the more inputs that come in, the more other suppliers who announce products cause all sorts of changes and you never actually get to a point when you can say that is what we will go and design. It is always 'where can we change this?'. Before you know where you are you have slipped six months. And you can't really afford to do that in this business . . . otherwise you don't get in to the key accounts . . . then you don't have enough business to sustain you.
>
> (Chief mechanical engineer)

> Management can't seem to make a decision. If they would make a decision and stick there, then you can go and design a specification, but the managers here don't seem to make decisions, they seem to like to go to meetings and sit around and argue, argue for hours, and come out with a decision that doesn't have any conclusion to it. . . .
>
> (Associate engineer)

The consequence of the 'me too' strategy, inadequately managed, was no product to sell.

Although recognising the need to become more efficient in design, marketing and production, Midas management had not created a structure which would enable it to compete on a 'me too' basis. Despite senior management trying continuously to drive costs down while increasing the pressure on development engineers to work to tighter deadlines for each successive product, new projects continued to exceed target costs and to be subject to considerable delay. It was evident during the fieldwork, and subsequently through continuing informal contact, that product development, despite being at the heart of the company's recovery strategy, was not proceeding well. Development activity was divided between two establishments, one in the USA and the other in the UK, each reporting to the vice president of engineering. It was carried out by electrical, electronic and mechanical engineers and structured around project teams headed by a senior engineer reporting to a development manager. The UK group, the main subject of this study, was managed by a recently appointed engineer. All engineers and the manager worked in the same open plan office, moving between shared workstations, test benches and their own desks. The engineers (twenty-one at the time of the study) were sub-divided according to specialism and assignment to projects, although, in practice, every engineer worked on each project as deadlines approached:

> There is a little bit of a strait-jacket on engineering here . . . it doesn't have a lot of sway. . . . The pressure on it is so intense that it can't sit back and think. . . . Every hour of every day it has to be producing, and producing, and producing.
>
> (Founder engineer)

Development timetables had become shorter and shorter, with development engineers routinely working overtime and still failing to meet deadlines. The products were no longer offering creative solutions to perceived technical problems. Despite formal procedures and structures to gather and feed back market intelligence into the development of products, in practice the structures were counter-productive. The replacement of leading edge with bleeding edge had not created a constructive dialogue over product design. Development had a feeling of working in a vacuum and certainly the younger engineers felt the lack of contact of any sort with customers. Although going through the motions of a formal development process, with its specified stages, in practice there was a sense of inertia, sometimes described as a death wish, in engineering:

> They're pushing things to the limit. They're expecting their engineers to

get every product to work and that's totally unreal. In any production you're going to have some sort of fall-out, that's automatic, but I think they expect me to come up with the goods every time. That constant pressure has had an effect on me, on my attitude towards the company . . . what's the point in me really trying to make the company succeed when I see that management doesn't really care about me? . . . Four or five years doing continuous overtime, under continuous pressure, doing this and that; it gets hectic, and there comes a stage where you say enough is enough and I can't really take any more of it!

(Design engineer)

Informal status hierarchies and the workplace or, how not listening to the market can be good for you

Ironically, one of the main reasons for this deep-rooted institutional malaise was that the company was trying to be responsive to customers, via perhaps the most common formal feedback loop: user intelligence gathered by marketing and customer support organisations. Instead of the prescribed equal dialogue between marketing, development and manufacturing, however, the development team was positioned at the bottom of the informal status hierarchy. Marketing had emerged at the top of this hierarchy as a result of the rhetoric of customer responsiveness and the strategy of trying to emulate more efficient suppliers. For development, marketing symbolised the difficult and elusive OEM customer, with its ever changing and ever increasing demands. Meanwhile a beleagured development could only struggle to respond and occasionally make jokes about the marketing manager – usually with a sardonic twist.

The informal status hierarchy afforded little room for manoeuvre to the development team and resulted in a defensive stance on their part. Beliefs about the team in the rest of the company were characterised by the manager as 'engineering produces trash'. Whatever the mistake or failure, development always seemed to be blamed: if the product could not be sold, it was development's fault; if the product could not be manufactured, it was development's fault. In effect, marketing became as much a buffer between development engineers and customers as it was a conduit of customer intelligence. The marketing department was small, staffed by people with a technical background but without the detailed technical experience of the development engineers. Their perceptions of customer needs – 'what the market wants' – were directed primarily to the development manager during meetings of senior company staff, and no effort was made by senior management to facilitate constructive dialogue between marketing and development. Marketing was seen as trespassing on development's territory by seeking to set design parameters and control development timetables. The general perception amongst the development engineers was that the company gave more weight to marketing than it did to their opinions on technical feasibility. In discussions about the technical performance of the drive, engineers had a standing joke about the marketing manager and his attempt to dictate specifications, which changed with every meeting. His surname was adopted in engineering diagrams as a new technical term describing performance characteristics of the drive.

The deadlines set were described by the development team as 'reverse engineered': that is, set by marketing, without their involvement, and determined by a date which marketing decided was when the product should be released in order to match the competition. Marketing was indeed acting as a conduit of user experience and needs into the company, but the traffic between the marketplace and Midas was entirely one-way; there was little open dialogue between customers and supplier here, but simply the presentation of technical features expected by customers, as seen through the eyes of the marketing manager. Development, from manager on down, felt themselves to be operating in a vacuum, lacking usable feedback from customers. The junior engineers felt they had no contact with customers of any kind:

> Feedback? Well, it doesn't exist.
>
> > (Design engineer)
>
> We don't get any feedback from marketing: it never filters down.
>
> > (Design engineer)
>
> They [management] are supposed to be the leading disk-drive technologists; they should be making the rules, or at least discussing them, and as to what the customer wants, who knows? Somebody must, but we don't see it.
>
> > (Design engineer)

From the perspective of development, marketing had power without responsibility, while they carried the responsibility for creating a viable design and meeting cost targets and deadlines. They were blamed for any delay, yet lacked the power to control the sources of delay (generally unforeseen technical problems or key suppliers failing to meet delivery dates). Marketing conversely could not understand why product development was so 'unreliable': they expected the tentative date set for release of product samples to be immovable and blamed the engineers when the date slipped or the sample device was technically incomplete. Marketing lost face with customers when it treated the date as hard and fast and promised the device to potential customers for inspection. Accusations flew back and forth: 'you said you'd do it and you didn't'. A succession of development managers had failed to establish a way of negotiating the uncertainties in their estimates. Marketing remained scornful of the engineers' attempts to discuss delays due to technical problems outside their control. The development engineers were correspondingly dubious about the skills of marketing, resulting in both sides alternating between defensiveness and arrogance.

The crucial organisational flaw was the lack of a properly structured connection between product design teams and marketing management, which could enable realistic discussion about the inevitable technical constraints on customer expectations. The result was that marketing was able to use its direct contact with customers as a legitimating device – who can argue against what the market wants, after all – and have the final say in timetabling and performance specifications. The development engineers knew the scheduling was unrealistic but were unable to alter it. They were condemned to an endless round of continuous overtime to meet externally imposed deadlines and an ever changing product specification, which in turn led to the open alienation of the engineers and a situation where, when interviewed, a very high proportion volunteered the information that they were actively looking for jobs elsewhere:

> One problem – and the 400 megabyte is a very good example – is that we can never decide what the specification for the product is going to be. There are sideways attacks from the marketing department and they don't know what they want. They visit a customer and come back and say, this is what they want, and then next week it has changed. There is no stabilising influence. . . . Very often they put unfair constraints on the engineering group. They might suggest what technology of head we use rather than just meeting the capacity. They might say, well, customer X likes to see thin-film data heads and very often they can actually wish to determine what technology is used in the drive, which I find very distressing at times.
>
> (Senior design engineer)

> In the past . . . engineering tended to produce the products and marketing had to go and sell them, and it was always the case that marketing would come back and say, if we had this feature we could sell more. So engineering got into this rut of enhancing products and capacities for customers, which didn't really cure the problems. Since the reshuffle of the company, marketing people now are asked, 'What do you want? We will create it and then you will have to sell it, because that is what you asked for' . . . but what marketing wants isn't easily attainable, technically. You can go to marketing and ask what they want in a three

and a half inch, and they say, give us 800 megabytes on a three and a half inch, we could sell that. But the technology to do that isn't quite here yet. It's not far away, but it's not here today ... the demands made by marketing are very ... they are out there in the front, they are pushing technology to the limits, in some cases beyond.

(Senior design engineer)

The difficulty of staying within tight schedules was further worsened by the ability of manufacturing to make repeated demands on development for help with routine production engineering, which interfered with the ability of development to set its own priorities. Perversely, this was particularly damaging to long-range development plans, which investigate the introduction of new materials and techniques into future products, because this tended to be the activity which was repeatedly postponed in favour of routine product support work. It could be argued that, for the development engineers, this in itself constituted a defensive move to avoid having to engage with difficult, new technical areas when the struggle to stay in the same place was already overpowering. Even if there was an element of avoidance, the inability to offset the demands of manufacturing was nevertheless particularly damaging for technical innovation.

The result of the customer-responsive ideology, its accompanying race to market mentality and the resulting informal status hierarchy was anxiety, strain, increasing labour turnover and poor performance: 'there is never enough time to do it properly but there is time enough to do it again and again and again' (design engineer). Contrary to conventional wisdom, Midas might have survived had it paid less attention to what its customers said they wanted.

CONCLUSION: USER FEEDBACK – SOME THOUGHTS ON GOOD PRACTICE

As the experience of our case study companies shows, the incorporation of user needs and experiences into the enhancement of existing products and the design of new ones is far more difficult than it appears at first sight. 'Giving the market what it wants' is an easy principle to pay lip-service to, but real business life is more complex than many textbooks and business school courses would have us believe. Nevertheless, some of the discussions and experiences we have looked at so far suggest that there are general principles about user feedback and company structure that the wise manager could take on board. They can be summarised as follows.

1　*Feedback loops are both formal and informal.* A supplier will only have a three-dimensional view of the marketplace when both formal and informal loops are used to gather information. This means actively seeking out forums through which company staff can meet industry colleagues, in other suppliers and users, on a regular basis.

2　*User feedback should be the basis for dialogue, not an end in itself.* As Midas plc's unhappy experiences demonstrate, when user experience sets technical parameters without the involvement of R&D staff in the supplier, the results can be disastrous. Dialogue between technical staff of users and suppliers can educate both, and should be an explicit motive behind the construction of feedback loops.

3　*There should be at least some direct contact between users and R&D experts.* Those development experts working for suppliers who provided at least occasional direct contact with users found it centrally important to their work. The formal feedback mechanisms for transmitting user experience, most notably marketing groups, do not always work. Sometimes they lead into management structures rather than R&D laboratories; sometimes they cannot carry the reaction to user feedback that should form the basis for technical dialogue between supplier and user. These pitfalls can be skirted by providing for direct contacts through customer visits, user group meetings or other means.

4　*Contact between marketing and R&D staff should be encouraged, by organisational reforms if necessary.* It is not enough for marketing and R&D staff to meet occasionally over a manager's table. Substantive user–supplier dialogue cannot take place without intense exchange of views between R&D and marketing staff in suppliers. At least some R&D and marketing staff need to work in the same building, preferably in the same room, and have meetings at frequent intervals. It is essential to involve both senior and junior staff in each department, to encourage exchanges of views at all levels.

5　*Management must give both marketing and R&D a hearing, and create formal reporting mechanisms to make this possible.* Dialogue between suppliers and users presupposes equal opportunities within suppliers for both R&D and marketing staff to present their opinions to management. Unless management follows an 'equal opportunities' policy in this respect, with both R&D and marketing personnel able to express worries and fears to managers through formal consultation procedures, user opinion will either be unduly privileged or ignored, depending on who has the management's ear.

4 Growing expertise

The user dilemma

Make or buy? The user's perspective

Is it more efficient for a firm to develop products or processes in-house, or externally by out-sourcing? With product markets perceived to be changing too rapidly for traditional solutions to work and economic policies in the Western world uniformly emphasising the 'discipline' of the market, the make or buy conundrum has increasingly become part of the policy agenda for senior managers. Because information technologies are perceived as enabling firms to respond quickly and flexibly to product markets, users have often reconsidered their approach to the development of in-house computing expertise, and sought instead a short-cut to systems development through collaborative projects with suppliers.

Suppliers themselves, keeping pace with product innovations, are reappraising their role in existing supply chains. Some senior managers are reassessing the extent to which each distinct area of production is central to the business: which activities add value to the materials at each stage of production? Hence computer systems suppliers such as Telewave Electronics (TE) were asking whether they needed to manufacture the plastic and metal shells or the cable harnesses for their systems, when they could subcontract this work more cheaply to a smaller firm. Conversely, loss of control over the design and production of key electronics components, so that supply is controlled by a small number of powerful firms, was regarded as a threat to long-term profitability. Smaller firms such as Midas, suppliers to the big computer systems manufacturers, have also been forced to become more selective about what aspects of the product they design and develop in-house. The growth of specialist suppliers, making system components, means that it is expensive and inefficient to control all specialist expertise internally. When everyone is using the same components, the dilemma over what should be maintained in-house becomes a question of identifying the core expertise which will allow one firm to differentiate its product from that supplied by the competition.

Overall the concerns of management, whatever the firm's location in the supply chain, can be captured under the umbrella of flexibility and the accompanying enthusiasm for the principles of total quality management (TQM). TQM can be regarded as a means of promoting 'entrepreneurial' activity among managers and experts in formerly bureaucratic, mechanistic organisations. To the extent that it focuses on processes of production and innovation, it raises questions about the quality of relationships between different functions, notably R&D, marketing, materials procurement and manufacturing, and provokes analysis of their role in facilitating or blocking innovation. A further consequence of TQM is to direct attention to supplier–customer relationships, both internal and external, and to emphasise the objective of meeting customer requirements. As a result, some firms have sought to externalise previously in-house services, or create quasi-market relationships internally, as well as seeking closer relationships with external suppliers.

For students of organisational behaviour, questions about the appropriate balance between in-house and external activity are relatively new. In the past the organisation and its environment have been treated as discrete, relatively enduring entities which interact in predictable ways. Most attention has been given to issues of divisionalisation and the relative efficiency of such structures. Conventional wisdom about the merits of the divisional form is currently being questioned: divisions themselves pursue sectional interests and may be unresponsive to redirections from the corporate centre (Hamel and Prahalad, 1989). At a more prosaic level, the uncertainties faced by managers about where the boundaries of their organisation should be drawn have not commonly been addressed. Consequently there is little empirical material on the types of trade-offs made by firms between development in-house and out-sourcing.

Industrial sociology has focused on the use of subcontracting as a means by which the core firm cuts costs, and hence passes risk down the chain onto smaller contractors. There are typically damaging consequences for labour in the smaller firms (Fevre, 1987; Phizacklea, 1990). Moreover contracting out is not a straightforward solution to control of labour and other costs if the consequence is reduced quality of product or service. Consequently, firms using subcontractors for work previously done in-house need to develop proactive vendor management, whereby they invest their own expertise in the supplier's process and product in exchange for greater control over quality, price and reliability. In other words, there is more to the decision about make or buy than a simple equation of relative costs and the construction of an internal contract for labour or an external contract for supply of goods and services.

Economists have had a longer historical interest in the question of make or buy, particularly exemplified in the work of Williamson (1975, 1986), whose discussion of markets versus hierarchies has received renewed attention in the light of the current political emphasis on the efficient operation of markets. Williamson, in keeping with the traditions of economics, has reverted to first principles to propose a general framework for the explanation of firm-level decisions about the balance between make or buy. He starts from the assumption that the market is pre-given and is economically rational. Human nature is treated as individualistic and instrumental; the problem of social control is resolved by means of contracts. The existence of organisations can be explained only in terms of their transaction cost advantages for certain activities. Transaction costs are the costs involved in developing and enforcing governance structures, especially contracts and hierarchies. A decision on whether to carry out work under market contract or organisational hierarchy is seen as determined by the relative costs of managing the work. He qualifies the economic rationality principle by positing that individuals (and organisations) act opportunistically, according to bounded rationality, and that actual decisions are contingent on the technical characteristics of the work, its complexity and the need for specialist knowledge. Williamson's analysis implies that in the long run task uncertainty, the requirement of frequent transactions, asymmetry of specialist knowledge and specificity of skills to the firm would all tend to favour in-house production, while routine, simple, non-specific tasks would favour market contracting.

In practice the behaviour of organisations is not in any simple sense economically rational, even though senior management may strive towards such a goal. As we have argued, what is perceived as rational, or profit maximising, is itself the subject of negotiation; there is no simple means for example of identifying the most profitable strategy, or guaranteeing its successful pursuit, given that organisations are constrained by their own history and cannot control the future. Williamson tends to assume that a clear differentiation can be made between the relative costs and benefits of market versus hierarchical solutions. In practice it is less straightforward. The market itself is likely to be less than perfect in meeting all requirements. Moreover, the definition of tasks to be contracted out is likely to be the subject of struggle between different interested groups. Williamson does give some recognition to this process by defining human nature as opportunistic and manipulative, but this gives only one side of the picture. Even if self-interest was the sole motivation for action, it is difficult to see how this translates directly into choices between market or hierarchical contracts.

There is some evidence for example that buying-in can be pursued successfully where a development is technically complex and regarded as strategic for the business but the organisation lacks the necessary expertise (Dyerson and Roper, 1991; Tierney and Williams, 1991). Our own conceptual framework implies that, in principle at least, firms should be able to manage uncertainty about the application of new technologies by collaborative developments with suppliers. Hamel and Prahalad (1989) argue that senior management should identify and enhance core competences in their business (rather than core products) and that one of the ways to do this is to form alliances with other firms who have a successful track record in a desired area of competence. They stress that this is not an argument for vertical integration by another name: 'managers deciding whether to make or buy will start with end-products and look upstream to the efficiencies of the supply chain and downstream toward distribution and customers' (p. 83). The resulting logic for vertical integration, they argue, would not look to the product range, but would create integration in those aspects of the chain which support core skills. Thus a company would not choose to cut internal investment in key areas unless it intended to cede control over the future technical direction of its products. The overall thrust of this argument undermines Williamson's general thesis that task uncertainty and firm-specific knowledge require a hierarchical structure of control and would suggest that the appropriate organisational form cannot simply be read off from the nature of the activity. In a period of continuing economic uncertainty, Williamson's framework appears relatively static. It cannot easily explain changes over time in the variety of structural recipes invented by firms to manage the uncertainties of competition. Nor can firms be confident that the current recipe will guarantee profitability.

This chapter and the subsequent one analyse interaction between and within firms over the uncertainties of make or buy, through two case studies of firms actively reappraising their business structures and strategies. The approach adopted assumes a degree of indeterminacy in the process of decision-making about the balance between in-house versus external sourcing. We are especially concerned with the ways in which the roles of managers and experts are affected by movement away from in-house control of innovation towards collaborative developments, or the buying-in of expertise. The nature of people's work is fundamentally altered when they become negotiators in a network of supply relationships, in team and project structures, rather than dealing with peers employed by the same firm. The distribution of costs and benefits between suppliers and customers is likely to be a much more conscious aspect of relationships than is the case for in-house developments, even where there is a tradition of profit centres at local level. We argue that a firm's success in the network depends partly on how key figures handle project management and conflicts, and partly on the relative power of the firm in the network.

Clearly, firms which are relatively dominant in their own markets are in a much stronger position to exert control over suppliers than are smaller firms who are dependent for survival on contracts to supply a few powerful customers. These smaller firms are unlikely to be able to command high levels of responsiveness from their own suppliers, who will prioritise their more powerful customers, yet they are far more constrained in their ability to be self-sufficient in all areas of their business. However, the balance of power in the network is mediated by the relative expertise of the firm's representatives in dealings with suppliers. Thus dominant firms are not exempt from the experience of dependence on an external supplier who is working on a project regarded as strategic to the business if there is little competition for supply and the customer lacks the relevant technical or managerial skills to develop an integrative relationship. Similarly the fate of smaller firms is not entirely determined by relative powerlessness in the supply network, but may be influenced by in-house competence or incompetence.

Our interest in expertise led us to focus on transactions between firms which require continuing involvement of skilled labour, where the technology is neither 'transparent' (instantly usable by most people) nor clear-cut in its application, and yet is regarded as a key component of the customer's products or processes. The first case, discussed in this chapter, is a large firm in a relatively dominant position in the food, drink and tobacco sector. Using principles derived from TQM, it is in the process of introducing integrated management information and production control systems across the company and is intensively courted by computer systems suppliers because of the potential value of its contracts. Here we focus on its moves to change the balance between in-house and external computing expertise. The second case, discussed in Chapter 5, is Midas, a medium-sized firm struggling to survive in a very competitive market. Its initial aim, described in Chapter 3, had been to develop and control its own technical expertise for the high-value end of the computer market. Its success meant that it wielded considerable authority over suppliers. Its declining business performance, however, meant that it became increasingly reliant on suppliers for favourable treatment. Despite a revised technical strategy, it struggled to retain control over its core mechanical and electronics expertise.

ALBION SPIRITS

We can use the story of Albion Spirits (AS) and its takeover by the international conglomerate Corporate Booze, as a real-world illustration of the problems of expertise management that we have so far mainly discussed in theory. It is a particularly good example of a company which has changed its approach to the make or buy dilemma. In 1985 it was a traditional, rather old-fashioned company with a benevolently paternalistic attitude towards its employees. It also had a long tradition of growing expertise internally. Five years later, it was well on the way to becoming an altogether different kind of business animal: 'leaner, fitter, hungry' for new business, but not the kind of company many of the pre-takeover employees could feel comfortable with. Along the way, it was evolving a company IT policy that marked a radical change with the past, inclining far more to buying-in and only cultivating selected areas of expertise internally. In terms of the impact on balance sheets, AS could be said to be making a successful business transition: profits and productivity have risen steadily since the Corporate Booze takeover. Senior management has a clear vision of what the company should look like in the future, and new IT systems are poised to play an important role in the company development. Yet the history of AS since its takeover by Corporate Booze has not been without problems, and in some ways, most notably in relations with employees, the company has paid a high price.

Textbooks caution against reading too much into a single case study, but only the wilfully blind could fail to see larger forces at work in what happened to AS. The takeover by Corporate Booze took place in 1986, a time when takeover activity in Britain was reaching a frenetic pitch. These were the peak years of the British boom of the mid-1980s, the time when the radical economic programme of the Thatcher premiership seemed to be working. Later on, it soured. Several of the most publicised results of the merger fever that swept the City of London in those years ended in tears, or in court. The AS takeover was never less than highly controversial, both at the time and since. Several of those behind it were involved in a celebrated court case; three ended up in prison. The Corporate Booze case became a symbol of the excesses of the Thatcher years, as established ways of doing business were overtaken by more ruthless methods which were in the short term economically effective but often seemed morally dubious. It is hard not to see what happened to AS, the dismantling of the old and its replacement by the cost-effective but less human new, as a potent metaphor of the kind of social and economic changes that took place in Britain during the Thatcher years.

At the company level, the transition AS underwent involved the restructuring of the two sets of relationship that make up the management of expertise. Internally, established centres of expertise had to be evaluated, their future planned and the relationship between centres changed. Senior managers had to decide which brands of existing expertise to retain and which to discard, as well as which new areas of expertise to grow within the company or buy in. These decisions were inseparable from specific IT purchasing decisions, as well as the process of organising acquisitions which underlaid individual decisions. They therefore necessarily involved a reordering of external relationships too, as senior management set about forging new relationships with a number of suppliers, contractors and consultants. As the effect of these changes was often to subcontract a technical function to an external third party, where the work would previously have been done in-house, much of the organisational change the company has undergone since 1986 can be understood in terms of the interplay between internal and external sources of expertise, and the attempt to find a satisfactory balance between them.

AS is a large company, with a turnover of approximately US$3.5 billion and employing 14, 000 people in Britain alone. It is a leading producer of alcoholic drinks, with several household name brands. Ironically, given the turn events would take in 1986, it had a history of expanding by the acquisition of smaller drinks companies. Before the takeover, according to those who survived into the Corporate Booze era, AS was a very clear example of what Burns and Stalker call a mechanistic company. Managers recalled it as hierarchical, paternalistic, conservative and not the place for young, ambitious types: 'very rigid structure, the only way you got X or Y's job was when he died!'; 'AS was a nice company, a good company to work for. Note the years we have all put in . . . but they hadn't got their IT act together at all, or their business act, come to that'.

In organisational terms the company was highly segmented. Although some services were provided at group level, primary production was organised into six brand companies, operating 'totally autonomously: the parent company had little idea of what was going on'. Each company had its own data processing (DP) department, and that department would run – or fail to run – a number of systems covering the entire range of company operations, from sales and marketing through production processes and planning to inventory control and invoicing. To use a political metaphor, the brand companies were nominally part of a federation, but were in practice self-governing. This independence had its advantages: the brand companies were perceived as friendly employers and traces of nostalgia were very evident in some reminiscences:

> I suppose something of the friendly brand company type image has been lost, but that hasn't been a bad thing for Corporate Booze or the shareholders. It has probably been a bad thing for a lot of the staff, because it was cosy to work in that way. And a lot of people haven't mentally made the transition, and never will, probably. It is apparent when you visit some of what were the brand companies . . . you still feel it when you go in, the old autonomy, it is still there. It shouldn't be, but it is . . . there is a cultural change which is still reverberating around.
>
> (Information services manager)

This lack of co-ordination of company activities at the group level was fully reflected in the organisation of IT acquisition. Although there was a central group data processing department, with a headcount of around fifty, it was highly segmented and very rigidly organised:

> It was a very structured environment. The career paths there were programmers, analysts, team leaders, managers; very clear reporting lines, very clear responsibilities . . . most people there were going up very traditional routes. Up the programming leg, programming team leader, then possibly transferring across because that was seen as a block, on to analysis and team leading and project management.
>
> (Middle manager)

The group DP department was never able to impose its will on the brand DP departments. The brand departments were able to protect their independence by referring to a company history of brand company autonomy – 'the companies had such autonomy in all areas of business and IT that they just did their own thing' – and ex-group DP managers were frank in their admissions of failure:

> I think there was an attempt to standardise on Acme Electronics equipment, but as to what authority we had to actually do anything in the line of policing, or even a QA [quality assurance] type role, I suspect it was done more by virtue of who the people were and the relationships they had managed to form with people.

> *What were relations like between you and the brand company DP shops?*

> We did have a lot of dealings, but largely through committees and working parties. I suppose . . . it was one of competition, and I don't think we were seen as any sort of service that they wanted. In fact, I think we were seen as being a thorn, trying to impose systems that they didn't want but were told they ought to have.

IT acquisition, viewed from the group level, was something of a disaster area. There was no co-ordination between brand company DP departments – there was no organisational mechanism through which DP managers in different brand companies could meet, for example, and one DP manager saw the production systems from another plant 20 miles away for the first time in 1990, after having worked with the company for sixteen years! Communication between systems was not an issue. There was enormous variation in the level of computerisation and computing expertise in different business units, with the typical situation being pockets of expertise in different areas, all fairly isolated from one another. A further problem was redundant expertise: IT specialists were skilled programmers in increasingly dated languages, notably Cobol, and tended to solve problems by writing code themselves. Naturally, this aversion to off-the-shelf packages made the problems of standardisation even worse. There was an attempt to monitor acquisitions and develop systems centrally via the group DP department, but the only practical legacy was the specification of a preferred hardware supplier at group level. Operationally, without effective policing this was too loose a directive to make much difference:

> Six different bottling plants and they had six different systems. Fair enough, most of them were running on Acme Electronics hardware, but the DP departments developed things differently, so that the systems were incompatible and therefore getting information was a nightmare ... we should have come up with a complete new set of systems, but they said, oh no, we've got people at each part of the plant who are paid differently, have different hours, etc.!
>
> (IT manager)

Perhaps the most glaring manifestation of bad business practice in IT policies was the emergence of the reverse of the technology champion – the 'technology blocker' – who actually managed to insulate strategic areas of the company's operations from computerisation well into the 1980s:

> Most accounting systems are computerised these days in big companies, and the company in charge of the grain distilling side had been looking at computerisation for over ten years, would you believe, without actually doing anything. I mean, they commissioned all sorts of studies and there was masses of paperwork, but nothing had happened ... the company secretary at the time didn't like the idea of computers, I think that was the truth of it, and resisted it.
>
> (Finance director)

There were other pockets of expertise at group level besides the group DP shop. Two in particular would provide very concrete problems in the management of expertise after the takeover. Engineering Services was, in the words of its director, 'quite straightforwardly a service department. People would come along and say, the decision has been taken to build a plant at site X with capacity Y, let's have a design and cost for it.' Research Laboratories occupied a site together with a quality assurance laboratory, and had a remit to pursue scientific analysis and research relevant to all stages of the group's operations, from raw materials through to the finished product in the bottle. It was left to itself to decide what analytical systems it wished to purchase. Functionality rather than compatibility was the main criterion for acquisitions, with the result that, as the director admitted, 'some of the older equipment we have got is not compatible within the building, never mind compatible with anyone else'.

The Corporate Booze takeover

To say that organisational reforms began as soon as the takeover was completed in 1986 rather understates the traumatic nature of the changes that were imposed. Senior managers left in droves: to take one example, the top four managers of the group DP shop were sacked the day after the takeover. AS began a period of intense structural upheaval, devised and supervised by a corps of new senior managers who were either attached to AS from other Corporate Booze business units or recruited externally. In terms of the political metaphor used above, the idea was to bring the unruly provinces of AS under tight federal control by creating new, centralising lines of managerial authority. Technology acquisition and the management of expertise in general are areas where the struggle between federalism and regional autonomy is still a live organisational issue.

AS, together with a smaller drinks company acquired by Corporate Booze shortly before the takeover, became one of three operating divisions within Corporate Booze. The others were Corporate Drinks, Corporate Booze's traditional core business, and Corporate Commercial, which grouped the various holdings that Corporate Booze had acquired as it diversified into the hotel and leisure sectors. The restructuring of AS could not have been more far-reaching: 'people left in their droves, totally changed; the whole focus was different'. Although the names of the old brand companies were retained, they were effectively dismembered and their various functions reordered into three cross-cutting business units. The largest is production, encompassing raw material purchases, distilling, stocks and domestic sales, and also including engineering and research laboratories. The export departments of the brand companies were amalgamated into a single central exports office, and finally the six bottling plants were brought together in a single bottling division. Although IT systems came in for some special organisational attention after the takeover, as we shall see, they were not a priority for the simple reason that the immediate organisational problems entailed in carrying the restructuring through were too pressing. For some time, both IT purchases and the setting of an IT strategy were put on the backburner, as the surviving DP managers in what used to be the brand companies struggled to come to terms with what the business reorganisation implied:

> We recognised quite early on that the structure of the systems that we were running was fairly inappropriate to the business organisation that we were now having to support, but the early attempts to change were really thwarted; because the business had this tremendous organisational problem to deal with, they really didn't want to have new computer systems to deal with at the same time. So, for the past eighteen months to

two years, what we have been trying to do, the emphasis has been on holding the thing together.

One of the unfortunate but inevitable consequences of the reorganisation was that technological chickens came home to roost. With the breaking up of the brand companies and the amalgamation of their functions, the patchiness of computerisation and the lack of standardisation in IT systems became a major problem for the new business organisation. Business units can be formed and reformed by executive fiat: computing systems, once installed, are less amenable to managerial instructions. The technical problems that were generated as a by-product of the reforms were considerable: functions were computerised in some plants and not in others; where computerisation had taken place, different plants developed systems individually to the point where linkages between systems were difficult or impossible; management in different plants had different methods for extracting information, and product identification codes were numeric in some plants and alphanumeric in others. Even the most basic management information was difficult to obtain, as a finance manager recalled:

> The whole thing was a complete shambles, you can imagine, with six branches literally all doing their own thing. There was a system established, and there was a manual to go with it, but they all had their own interpretation . . . the first set of accounts that I actually looked at were absolute nonsense, I mean, just rubbish, variances all over the place, they just didn't make any sense at all.

Of the established centres of specialist expertise, Research Laboratories was the least affected by the reorganisation. Although it now came under the administrative purview of production, its remit was unchanged and it suffered no internal restructuring or changes in headcount. Engineering's role was expanded after 1968: its headcount rose from forty-five to sixty-three between 1989 and 1990 alone. Its remit was widened to include planning of re-siting needs and the monitoring of technical engineering requirements for both production and bottling. Chemical engineers service production, mechanical engineers bottling, while electrical, construction and project engineers serve both.

One new development for Engineering was in automatic process control instrumentation. This is an area which has undergone a technical revolution over the last decade, with digital instruments replacing earlier electronic and pneumatic models. Before 1989 there was not a single automatic process control technologist in Engineering, but four were recruited that year to bed down a distributed process control system acquired for a distillery. This acquisition, which cost US$1.4 million, would bring Engineering into direct contact with the most visible organisational evidence of the effect the takeover had had on the management of IT systems and technology acquisition generally: a new IT department set up immediately after the takeover, called Information Services.

Information Services: managing internal expertise

Information Services grew out of a historical accident. About a year before the AS takeover, a senior executive of Corporate Booze began an initiative to restructure IT acquisition policies by establishing Information Services. Its remit was to provide technical computing assistance to the component operating divisions. It was to work within a general IT development framework drawn up at senior management level. In practice, it had two interconnected roles. The first, operational assistance to business units, although technically complex, was politically less problematic than the second: it included technology assessment, involvement in negotiations with suppliers, end user training and some software development. Where political problems were more likely to crop up were in its associated role in monitoring technology acquisitions. In certain circumstances this might involve a policing role where a particular acquisition went against the requirements of the IT development framework.

With the takeover, new management was grafted onto the decapitated DP department and it became the Information Services group serving the AS operational division within Corporate Booze. As AS concentrated on distilling and Corporate's core business was brewing, there was little overlap between AS's Information Services unit and information services in Corporate Booze. Although AS's Information Services head reported to a Corporate Booze board member, Information Services within AS was left to implement policy without interference from corporate level. The newly imported senior Information Services management organised the department by creating accounts for each of the three AS business units and allocating account managers to them. Below senior levels, it was staffed mainly by people who had worked either in the old group DP unit or one of the six brand-name DP units.

Thus Information Services represented by far the most important internal reservoir of IT expertise at AS. It was also the crucial organisational link between AS and IT suppliers, as well as other third parties such as consultants and software houses. In other words, Information Services is the sharp end of the management of expertise at AS. It is through its mediation that the balance between internal and external sources of expertise is to be found and IT policy implemented. Specifically, it was to a large extent the senior management of Information Services which decided what IT skills needed to be retained by the organisation and which could be bought in. It also had a pressing problem of redundant expertise, as many of the programmers and computer analysts were more DP professionals than information engineers, and their skills were geared towards centralised mainframe information processing rather than the distributed computing and area networks that increasingly define modern IT. In the short term, it was not necessary to be a computer expert to realise that there were major economies which could be made through improving co-ordination in computing, partly by standardising future IT acquisitions and partly by improving information flows in installed systems. The degree of control and standardisation that Information Services could impose on business units became an important organisational issue. Several Information Service managers, with their backgrounds in DP departments in the old brand- name companies, understood very well the tradition of regional self-rule and pockets of expertise that would complicate their jobs from now on. One of those ex-DP shop managers who transferred to Information Services defined its dual role as follows:

> To deliver in a sensible fashion . . . IT systems and services to the business community, quite simply, and really to act in a monitoring or policing role where the business may be . . . going off at a tangent to what Information Services see as being a correct framework within which the business should be working.

Since 1986, Information Services has indeed had some trouble in breaking down traditions of regional autonomy and policing IT acquisitions by established centres of technical expertise within AS. The most problematic acquisitions were those by Engineering and Research Laboratories, where it was possible for managers to argue that they had particular kinds of IT expertise within these units which Information Services did not possess. This automatically created problems in Information Services' relationship with bottling, since bottling also had long-established dealings with Engineering and had traditionally drawn upon it for particular kinds of engineering expertise. With the general move towards digital systems in the 1980s, by the time of the takeover Engineering had developed some expertise in industrial process automation. It was therefore natural that bottling turned to Engineering rather than to Information Services for initial technical help in developing an automated plant maintenance system in one of the bottling plants. As it turned out, the system Engineering opted for was a Corporate Booze standard package and Information Services was brought in to handle dealings with the supplier, but Information Services account managers were not happy with the fact that they were not called upon until the project was already well advanced:

[Engineering] are another organisation on the side, and they provided a solution for one of the bottling plants, for instance, for plant system involvement, and we could argue there, but we were not particularly involved in that one. It was one of the ones that was presented as a *fait accompli* and the only thing you could do was say yes or no.

The acquisition of a US$1.4 million automatic process control system threw the problem of how to organise the division of computing and engineering expertise into even starker relief. While recognising that Engineering was developing IT expertise in this particular field, Information Services account managers argued that technical competence was only half of the issue; business considerations were at least as important:

> To some extent they [Engineering] have run their own projects, considering themselves expert, and they are expert in many areas. They are as qualified to recommend a local area network and a minicomputer, say, in research and development, as we are. But there are other factors to deal with, in terms of integration, perhaps, and consistency.

If this acquisition was any guide, integration was a concept Engineering had some difficulties in taking on board. When the process control engineer in charge of implementing the project was asked, together with his superior, about their dealings with Information Services, they argued that Engineering had historically been responsible for 'project work for production plant control', and said that they had been dealing with Information Services 'not in a deep way, more as a guidance exercise ... we are trying our best to co-operate and understand their viewpoint of how the development should take place'. We gained a strong impression that the two spoke to each other occasionally, rather than maintaining systematic contact. A telling sign was that the sales representative of the system supplier, a man with over twenty years' experience of selling to AS, had not met any Information Services staff at any stage of the acquisition, despite being involved from pre-tendering to post-implementation.

In this acquisition, Information Services was primarily concerned with how the process control system was to be linked with management information systems, and felt its minimal involvement was the product of a breakdown in communications somewhere along the chain of managerial command. To the Information Services manager most directly involved, the incident acted as a spur to settle the question of jurisdiction with Engineering:

> Engineering are aware of where they are working with process control computers, and trying to strip data out for presentation to management information systems. They are not involved in that: I am. And that's why we need to communicate. I am quite happy that they have their projects

and that they run with their projects, but it is the communication thing I am not happy with. . . . I don't think there was any pre-definition of responsibility between Engineering and Information Services.

From Engineering's side, as expressed by a senior engineering manager, this appears like empire-building, an intrusive attempt to increase federal control over production, historically Engineering's responsibility whether the technologies involved were IT or not:

> Information Services . . . haven't spent a great deal of time in production process control to date. They have been working mainly on the fringe of the production department, interests in accounting, personnel, and now in plant maintenance, computing and things like this. . . .

In a way, Information Services has fallen victim to its own rhetoric about providing a business service. As a result, engineers believe Information Services' expertise is biased towards 'business' functions, which means it can be kept out of 'production', where engineers comfortable both with selected ITs and engineering problems can be left to plough their own furrow, much as they did before the takeover. The problem that Information Services faces is not just one of communication, but of philosophy.

What lies behind the ideal of providing a business service is not a separation of business from production – in this sense the engineering view is very traditional, referring back to an idea of organisations as segmented and mechanistic – but the belief of senior management in Information Services that modern IT means the collapsing of traditional barriers between production processes and business functions. With the radically new possibilities opened up by networking and information flows between systems organised along distributed computing lines, the information base exists for the implementation of production process reforms like just-in-time, TQM and so forth. Therefore, the worldview behind the 'business service' rhetoric asserts, it no longer makes sense to see an IT strategy as something which can be isolated from business strategy or production processes: all three must form an integrated whole if the company is to practise what senior Corporate Booze management preaches. IT expertise, therefore, should be like blood in the human body, carried to all parts of the commercial organism, with Information Services acting as the veins and arteries, providing the delivery system that links business units and circulates information between them – with senior managers making up the cerebral cortex, transmitting instructions and formulating strategy. Dividing IT expertise up into segregated specialisms, each allocated to a different business unit, is the antithesis of this organisational philosophy.

In the same way as engineers drew upon their specific historical tradition of expertise to buttress their autonomy, Research Laboratories attempted to underpin their pre-takeover autonomy in IT purchases by reference to a divide between scientific research and commercial computing – and to one of the most irreducible traditions of regional autonomy to be found anywhere in AS. The director seemed little concerned with issues of integration and standardisation of IT acquisitions when questioned about the degree of control he had in acquiring IT systems:

> We tend to be fairly self-contained. We can't say we don't have a need to link in with other parts of the business, but essentially, because we are research laboratories, we are the main centre for that in the company. I think we would have been able certainly to put forward a strong case for choosing the system that we wanted.

Research Laboratories has a strong emphasis on chemical research, and thus has a much narrower base of IT expertise than Engineering. In reality it came down to one person, jokingly but significantly described as 'a chemist gone wrong', who developed an interest in computing systems related to laboratory research. When Research Laboratories decided to update its obsolescent laboratory information management system (LIMS) in 1988, the computing chemist turned for back-up not to Information Services, with which he had had no contact, but to Engineering, with which he had worked before and where he knew the technicians personally. Research Laboratories, together with Engineering, drew up a tender and evaluated bids to install a LIMS. It was only when the system had been selected – or, in the words of the computing chemist, 'we had chosen our preferred solution' – that it went to senior management for final budget approval, and Information Services became aware of its existence.

An Information Services account manager was brought in at this stage, and from the Research Laboratories side the consultation was seen as unproblematic:

> Fred Bloggs was the contact at Information Services and he was first off with the documentation. We had one or two meetings just to answer any questions that he had, but effectively they had no concerns and they thought that our ... procurement exercise had been conducted in an extremely well-planned and organised fashion, and had no adverse comments to make, quite the contrary. Extremely pleased with the way things had been done.
>
> (Director, Research Laboratories)

Fred Bloggs's recollection of the episode, however, was rather different:

> At the eleventh hour we were asked to take a view on the LIMS, where it

was a *fait accompli*, it was done. When they were going for final approval, someone said, well, what is the Information Services view on this? And they said they didn't have a view, we haven't asked them! So we were quickly asked to give the nod, which isn't the correct way to be involved, obviously. That was one of the projects which pointed out the need to get involved a bit more with Engineering. LIMS was one they undertook on their own, and it was all right, it wasn't serious, but it could have been a totally different view from what we would have recommended by looking at the [IT].

An indication of the looseness of contact between RL and IS was that the director of RL could not remember at what stage Information Services has been involved in the acquisition. The director of RL constructed a divide between research and commercial or business activities, in the same way as Engineering fenced off production processes as its domain, in order to justify the exclusion of Information Services from purchasing decisions. Information Services, concerned with the relationship between sites rather than with sites *per se*, are perceived as IT generalists in business units which have a strong tradition of specialist expertise that encompasses some types of IT system.

Basically, [Information Services] were not too interested in it [the LIMS acquisition] because again it is a sort of specialised operation, as against them, who are basically a commercial computing business . . . they are not so much a production control set of people as a commercial set. So they wouldn't have felt they had the expertise to deal with the sort of lab requirements that we were looking at.

(Director, Research Laboratories)

Although Information Services did have difficulties in drawing jurisdictional boundaries with historically established centres of expertise, and in forcing the level of involvement in purchasing decisions to which it was theoretically entitled, it would probably be fair to regard these difficulties as the teething problems inevitable after such a wide-ranging business reorganisation. One of the reasons Information Services was involved at such a late stage in the LIMS, plant maintenance and automatic process control acquisitions was that in monetary terms they were not large enough to provoke senior management into monitoring the acquisitions from an early stage. Where the sums of money involved were large, as we shall see, Information Services did play the co-ordinating role envisaged for it since 1986. A series of meetings was held between Engineering and Information Services management during the latter phase of fieldwork to understand their respective remits and define ground-rules for future operations. It is too early to say whether further disputes will recur between Information Services and Research Laboratories or Engineering.

In the long term, it seems likely Information Services will bring the other centres of IT expertise in the company to heel, for two reasons. First, the traditions of regional autonomy are on the wane, as the acrimony of the takeover becomes part of an increasingly distant past and the benefits of the reorganisation on business performance become more apparent. Second, and at this point we can move from passive to active models of the management of expertise, other IT acquisitions that Information Services is in the process of co-ordinating are likely to precipitate the kind of organisational changes which will make the life of its managers a great deal easier. They also demonstrate how important relationships with suppliers and third parties can be in orchestrating organisational change, and the practical problems posed by the fact that new IT systems often require new skills. At one level it is misleading to present the user dilemma in the management of expertise as 'do we make or do we buy in', since skills are commodities that come in a human wrapper. For the employees, the dilemma becomes 'do we retrain or are we fired?' Inevitably, given the nature of IT systems, more people are fired than reskilled.

In the judgement of senior Information Services management, AS has now overcome the immediate organisational problems generated by the restructuring of the business, allowing them to play a much more active role in using IT systems to precipitate organisational change. This is reflected in the three largest projects that Information Services is currently involved with, all of which attempt to break down once and for all the organisational legacy inherited from the takeover. All three are integrating, cross-functional systems designed to pull AS into a federal management structure where the very idea of regional autonomy would be made unthinkable. By the mid-1990s, the strategy supposes, all business units will be linked together via IT systems which will produce the sophisticated information base that will enable the company to respond immediately to changes in market conditions. Each is being planned and implemented in a way which could not be more different from the pattern of IT development before the takeover.

At one level it reflects a shift from a make to a buy-in approach to the management of expertise, manifested in the involvement of a number of new suppliers and other external sources of expertise. However, it also reflects a deeper organisational change. Rather than the initiative for the acquisition of an IT system coming from a relatively autonomous centre of expertise in AS, it is coming from senior management at Corporate Booze and Information Services, concerned above all with the relationships between business units. The planning and tendering, in all three cases, is being co-ordinated by Information Services but organised on a project team basis orchestrated, in a move that would have been unthinkable in the recent past, by outsiders – consultants. Finally, each of the three projects is several orders of magnitude greater than previous IT acquisitions by AS, in terms of the amount of money Corporate Booze intends to spend.

The three projects are all medium rather than short term, planned to take between three and five years to complete. They are the creation of a group-wide product database; the construction of an integrated network allowing AS to manage its supply chain by linking it into joint venture partners and distributors; and the replacement of the jumble of manufacturing systems that currently exists in the six bottling plants with a single production system, allowing common working practices to be introduced across the bottling division. Each of these projects is in reality a large number of sub-acquisitions, involving the forging of relationships not just with hardware suppliers but also with software suppliers, software development and maintenance houses, consultants, contractors and subcontractors. Even had senior management wished to retain the historically established collaborative relationship with Acme Electronics, which it did not, the systems being acquired are so wide-ranging, and depend on such a number of separate specialised brands of expertise, that no single supplier could hope to corner the business. Each of these projects also clearly demonstrates the way senior management hoped to exploit new information technologies to create an integrated operational division where previously there had been a number of separate, and occasionally competing, business units.

Nevertheless, there are two problems which the company will need to address over the years to come. The least serious in organisational terms, although by far the most important on other criteria, is the inevitable alteration it will involve in the internal skills base in the company – or, in starker terms, the significant number of employees who will become surplus to requirements once implementation begins. This is already apparent in the most advanced of the three projects, the common manufacturing system being introduced in the bottling division. The project manager defined the implications for many clerical workers:

> We are moving from a company where the departments are very much operated by their own internally integrated system. Instead of you having a lot of clerical transferring of information on paper, it will be given to the system . . . there will be manning savings, and I think you will see it in that the level of clerical work doing the detail changes. I'll give you a parallel instance that I experienced when I was at Acme. We put in a new accounting system, computerised . . . the staff were in some cases a lot of women who each month had calculated the value of production and done it all as a clerical operation. All of a sudden we automated that; all you

did was feed in the information and the machine did it all. Their job was then to check what came out, but they weren't up to that. A lot of them never adjusted to that. They were fine with an old adding machine or a calculator, but to look and interpret was not a skill they had. Now I think we're starting to find the same situation here; your skill level changes and you need people who can look for something that is not right and then investigate . . . [you] can't retrain everyone, but we try to upgrade their level from being a doer to an interpreter, and then the ability to see a thing through, that you see a problem and investigate it.

Although it is difficult to put a number to it, it is clear that full implementation of these systems will involve considerable job losses, as long-established types of internal expertise become redundant. This does not just apply at the level of clerical workers; it is equally relevant to many programmers and analysts who used to work in the DP shops and now find themselves with IT skills which the speed of technological change in the IT sector is leaving behind. Indeed, part of the justification for the acquisition of these new systems is precisely that they will reduce labour costs and increase productivity. However, in AS, to paraphrase Orwell, all skills are redundant, but some skills are more redundant than others. Clerical workers are likely to find that they are laid off on a relatively large scale, but those who have redundant IT skills will probably find themselves being retrained, to make up an internal reservoir of IT expertise targeted on the specific technologies defined by senior management as strategically important. The reason for doing so leads into the second problem AS will have to confront: managing its external relationships in such a way as to buy in expertise as and when needed, without becoming entirely dependent on third parties for expertise in areas vital to company operations.

The main way in which a balance is being sought between internal and external sources of expertise is by the aggressive management of relations with suppliers. Underlying this, in its turn, is the shifting of information services to a central role in IT acquisition, allowing it to supervise all stages from planning through tendering to implementation and beyond. The mechanism through which this is being attempted is the setting up of project teams to draw up specifications and handle negotiations with suppliers. These project teams are made up of representatives from middle management in the bottling plants affected, one or two Information Services representatives to provide technical back-up and, crucially, a number of consultants holding the ring and co-ordinating business planning. The project teams work within parameters set by the Corporate Booze board member responsible for, and the head of, Information Services. The latter drew up the list of six suppliers who were to be invited to tender.

As a result, the pre-takeover situation where AS obtained most of its IT equipment from a long-term collaborative relationship with a single supplier, Acme Electronics, has been replaced by a wider portfolio of suppliers competing against each other in what the head of Information Services calls 'strategic terror':

> Suppliers [are] coming in and talking about strategic partnerships. Well, that's fine and dandy, but what they are actually doing is selling a mechanism to negate the fact that they don't have any differentiation between themselves in terms of price, performance, operating systems and portability. So the only way they can do that is get closer into bed with you. Now, if there is something tangible on the end of that that you get as a result, fine. But I think that all of the things that they could give you as a result of the strategic partnerships can be obtained as a result of strategic terror. If you keep them on their toes, they will respond to you as an active account.

While Information Services, with backing at Corporate Booze board level, has now managed to institutionalise its control of IT acquisition through project teams, it still has to face the problem that in certain areas, because of the pattern of technological innovation in the IT sector, it cannot avoid dependence on a single supplier without having the option of playing it off against a competitor. This is a consequence of the 'balance of expertise' referred to in the previous chapter. The strategic dilemma which over-dependence on a single external source of expertise represents is embodied in a supplier called Delphi, which has developed a particular information engineering technology. There is a consensus among IT experts both inside and outside Information Services that information engineering is the future in IT developments in this particular field, and it is set to play an important role in the development of IT systems in the medium term. Unfortunately for its users, information engineering is a classic example of supplier dominance over users in the marketplace during the early stages of innovation. It represents a qualitative technical improvement, but Delphi has a long lead in its development and it will be a considerable time before there are alternative sources of supply.

This means that AS will not be able to avoid depending on a single external source of expertise in a strategically important area, without having the option either of growing internal expertise or terrorising Delphi with the threat that they will switch suppliers. Simply put, AS is over a barrel, and this is not an uncommon situation for users to find themselves in. All the sophisticated ways of managing supplier relationships break down at the frontiers of IT development, the very areas where the promise of acquiring competitive edge in the marketplace is most real. Paradoxically, good management of expertise becomes most difficult when it is most commercially rewarding, because the structure of user–supplier relationships is biased towards the supplier at the exact moment when users most want the technology – when few competitors have it. It was hardly surprising, then, that the head of Information Services, should express a certain unease about the relationship with Delphi, in marked contrast to the ebullient self-confidence that characterised his descriptions of other supplier relationships:

> Delphi I find a very difficult relationship . . . because we have a statement of direction with regard to how we are going to use Delphi. So it worried me, because as a result I see we do not get the performance that as a customer spending a million dollars plus worldwide with their organisation, we should have much more added value from them, which we don't get. They see us as, oh yes, we'll send them another three copies of their database, or whatever. And I don't know how we get round that. We are strategically bound to Delphi. They know it and I know it.

These are the immediate problems AS will have to confront as it attempts to balance internal against external sources of expertise. It is too early to say how successful it is likely to be: all three projects are still in their infancy. In conclusion, however, it is worth noting that there is a third problem the company faces which may prove to be even more intractable than the other difficulties examined above. It relates to the general economic climate at the time senior management devised the IT development framework and planned a medium- to long-term acquisition programme. Times were easy on both sides of the Atlantic: high growth rates were reflected in microcosm on the swelling balance sheets of both AS and Corporate Booze. Indeed, it was that very availability of capital in the mid-1980s that was the precondition of the takeover fever which led Corporate Booze to gobble up AS. The IT acquisitions AS is making are expensive, despite their cost benefits, but are taking place in a recessionary economic climate. Recession is a severe test of the philosophy of integration of IT and business strategies. In AS as in other companies harder economic times may lead to the scaling down of IT development, which has in the past been one of the first things companies have cut when forced to draw in their horns. It is in a recession that we see whether companies have undergone a genuine change in business philosophy or whether the rhetoric of integration is, when the crunch comes, so much hot air.

5 Market power and the mismanagement of expertise

MIDAS

The story of Midas's rise and fall was begun in Chapter 3. Its history is in many ways a story of the change from attempted autonomy to attempted constructive interdependence. Here we examine the political process of managing expertise during a period when the firm could no longer afford to maintain sole control over product development. Instead, it was seeking to balance internal and external sources of expertise without damaging the distinctiveness of the product. We also aim to show how loss of market power influences the trade-offs between make or buy, and to examine the role of engineers and managers in the handling of suppliers when market power is in decline.

The Midas case demonstrates our basic argument that underlying the quasi-rational market calculations about make or buy is a non-rational structure of beliefs about what type of business you are in, how good you are in that field and how the business should be run. These beliefs are historically based, difficult to change and permeate the unwritten norms of company conduct. They are only partly amenable to rational influence in the form of feedback from the market or other outside observers. Such beliefs form a crucial part of the framework within which decisions about make or buy are made. We cannot understand why a company makes the trade-offs it does without understanding the contingent logic of these beliefs. First we describe the belief set which characterised Midas management in its early and middle period of operation and show how it became increasingly damaging to the viability of the company. We call the belief set The 'Midas syndrome': belief in the unassailability of the company; the belief that management could do no wrong; the belief in complete autonomy of expertise and the view that product development is a matter of basic skills plus common sense. These beliefs were associated with the application of a 'bomber crew mentality' to the development of new products; permanent orientation to the short term;

the absence of any structure to facilitate continuous development of new expertise, in either management or technical specialisms; the absence of an inbuilt critical capacity which would force periodic reappraisal of strategy; and, finally, the intense ego involvement of senior management in the current path. Second, having shown the damaging effects of this belief system and its associated practices, we examine the recent restructuring of product development and show how, despite the espoused total quality management strategy, the failure to overcome historical norms effectively ensured the demise of the company.

The stance of Midas's founder engineers was, necessarily perhaps, one of stubborn conviction in their own ability to start a high-tech company and develop a genuinely innovative product, in what was felt to be an anti-entrepreneurial climate. In the view of the founders, they were unsupported by the key development agency, who were suspected of lacking relevant business skills and of protecting the interests of multinationals over and above local enterprise. Given that one of the agency's roles was the support of foreign direct investment, it was felt to be reluctant to encourage senior executives to leave an existing multinational to start up a business in competition. There was also amongst the engineers a feeling of national pride:

> The four of us were basically running a plant which had a very good record of technology introductions . . . and what we were designing and manufacturing here was actually being gobbled up by the parent company. . . . So in 1979 the four of us which constituted the general manager, the technical manager, the manufacturing manager and the financial manager decided that they would like to go away and try and start a company of their own.
>
> (Founder)

After a year of somewhat clandestine meetings, venture capital was raised from 3i and the business began in 1980. A marketing manager was recruited, extending the founding group to five. After a period of intensive development work, the first product was shown at the USA Computer Convention in Chicago the following spring. The initial massive success of the company no doubt contributed to a belief in their infallibility:

> I used to have a feeling at that time that when we were thinking of things, it is almost like the self- fulfilling thing, our generation were just coming out of the 70s, starting to realise that the more power to your . . . you could always make your dreams come true. Certainly at that time you had that impression that if you do something strongly enough, work at it hard enough, that it will finally come true.
>
> (Founding member)

This was accompanied by strongly held convictions in the skills and judgement of the founding team and their ability to act in complete autonomy to create the best technical solutions. Textbook knowledge was eschewed in favour of common sense rules of thumb; external investment in software tools and new technologies was avoided. They prided themselves on being able to produce cheap, down to earth solutions to problems of technical enhancement which existing knowledge treated as insoluble.

> We tried to get blood out of a stone all the time. Our view was rather than spending £60,000 on this piece of equipment and £100, 000 on that, let's calculate and use our intuition and guess what the result is going to be rather than measure your way to the result . . . we didn't want to spend a lot of money on R&D and life is too short to do lots of academic exercises. We simply said right, it sounds intuitively right that we should do this, this and this. Let's do it.
>
> (Founding member)

When the changing market, recession and severe competition eventually resulted in the collapse of sales, the money in the bank disguised the reality of Midas's declining performance for some time. The intense ego involvement of the directors, and their belief in their infallibility, meant that they continued to operate under the delusion that the company was bound to succeed regardless of external changes. Despite the increasing technical complexity of the drive, they failed to develop new resources to match the competition or to make use of external expertise in areas of technical deficiency. Development work was completed by means of a 'bomber crew mentality': engineers were pushed to extremes to meet shorter and shorter deadlines. The vice president of engineering succinctly characterised the directors in this era as 'leading with the wrong part of the anatomy', with an accompanying 'closed, macho and maniacal' management style. The directors were spending more of their time criss-crossing the globe than they were dealing with the day to day realities of a crumbling business.

The changing shape of the industry

> A disk-drive designer . . . really is like a chef, he takes all the ingredients and he makes something very special. Now what is happening is these ingredients are becoming more and more sophisticated and for him to take more and more sophisticated parts and try and put them together becomes harder and harder.
>
> (Chief technical officer)

No outsider could fail to be impressed by the engineering skills which result in the transformation of abstract mathematics and schematics into a reliably functioning disk drive. Even the most jaundiced engineers were not immune to the excitement of seeing abstract design translated into material artefact. Making a disk drive which will function in another manufacturer's computer is by definition dependent on a series of collaborative relationships, internally as well as externally. Design engineers, specialised suppliers, customers and standards committees form a network which shapes the product from the mechanical form, through the design of the printed circuit board (PCB), the servo system and the specification of heads and disks to the data channel and interface with the computer. The industry has always comprised interdependent, specialised suppliers, operating in what was, only ten years ago, a very lucrative market. Latterly continuing recession has affected the viability of the industry, which has become increasingly concentrated, with fewer firms dominating more of the business. Fierce competition has cut, if not obliterated, profit margins and the trading atmosphere has soured: charges of corruption and fraudulent practices are not uncommon.

The growing emphasis on the ability to develop a product speedily, at relatively low cost, to high-quality performance standards has made relationships with suppliers a particular source of tension: 'it is one big unhappy family, everybody is fighting with each other but they are all helping each other' (chief mechanical engineer). Relationships with key vendors have to be actively managed, because they are able to determine the progress or otherwise of internal development timetables. An unresponsive supplier can undermine the credibility of the development team *vis-à-vis* marketing and manufacturing.

Although Midas had always been dependent on external suppliers of specialised components, over time the balance between make or buy had shifted distinctly towards buying in. There was a level at which Midas had no choice, because it lacked the resource base to do otherwise. But the structure of the supply chain had also changed, with the growth of specialist suppliers aiming to dominate the development and production of certain high-tech components of the drive. A number of suppliers had begun to move into the areas of expertise previously dominated by firms such as Midas, to provide black-boxed (or silicon-imprinted in this case) solutions to electronic problems of the drive. In the data channel area for example a small number of companies now provide all the various chips required:

We have integrated some of the stuff ourselves but the way the trend probably is I would say is to go to a specialised company to buy devices. There is still a lot of engineering to do to get these devices to work. There are a lot of external components to go round them and there are a lot of different things you can do, different techniques for using these black boxes. But principally their functions are defined and fairly well known. The trick is to integrate them into your specific application.

(Principal engineer)

Midas had originally designed most of its own integrated circuits, but cost and time pressures had worked to determine that these were now bought in, as general purpose devices, to be customised later. Fully customised devices, which tended to be developed collaboratively, were expensive but efficient in the use of silicon. Their main disadvantage was that they took ten to twelve weeks to produce. For Midas engineers, collaboration with vendors meant using the supplier's design facilities, because Midas lacked the appropriate modelling software. This had its advantages – expertise was on hand to help resolve technical problems – but it also meant that, having used the facilities, the engineer felt committed to that supplier. Latterly, the interface between drive and computer, which carries many integrated functions, was also beginning to be manufactured as a single black box solution by vendors. In this area, however, Midas had held back from the buy-in option, because of the perceived strategic importance of the interface to the character of the end product. The interface is the most visible feature of the drive from the customers' point of view:

This is the front end . . . everybody has to talk to the drive through this interface and there is a lot of diagnostic stuff. . . . There has to be a lot of close-cut collaboration between all the groups to get things working.

(Principal engineer)

It is the focus of compatibility issues, where what appears to be a precise technical definition is nevertheless negotiable:

We work to a spec for this interface, but there are different interpretations of a spec, different emphasis that people put on various parts of the spec, and if a customer goes down one path of one vendor he will come to expect things to work in a certain way, expect certain functions to be available. And if we come up with a similar drive that is compatible, he expects those functions to be exactly the same. They may not be. . . .

(Principal engineeer)

The micro code for the interface had received increasing attention, reflected in higher levels of resources and, more informally, in the higher status attached to micro-code developers in the department. The work is seen as difficult, involving the generation of a volume of code which is in turn difficult to test.

In general the trend by the chip manufacturers to integrate more of the electronics was likely over time to externalise more of the work originally done in-house. Midas's chief technical officer saw this as a trend which should be capitalised on:

> What I think should be done now is [the engineer] should start to do some more macro-design, like the chef that says, right, the dough for this – you will make the dough; and all the decorations on the top – you are the expert on this. I think the disk-drive designer now should be . . . working with other people who are experts outside. And say look I've got this great idea, what I want to do is such and such and you're the expert on it so why don't we do a little consultative thing, then we'll buy it back from you, rather than, as has been our tradition of sitting down and saying right this motor has to have the following specification and we write the spec and give it to the motor designer and he goes and makes it. . . . Then it doesn't work and we get into the usual fight and eventually it does work.

There were advantages to increasing interdependence. To the extent that other specialists developed part of the drive that Midas lacked the resource for, the technology was pushed forward and Midas benefited. Such suppliers were widely held to be the best sources of information on new developments and new technologies: 'the best way (to keep up to date) is to visit the vendors regularly . . . you can learn more on a three day visit to ABC than you could by reading the technical publications every month' (project manager). Partnerships with vendors were the source of inspiration and awareness:

> The head guys are away inventing heads and they want outlets for their new ideas as well, so they are interested in getting partnerships. Similarly with the chip guys. They have a big problem in that they're trying to meet everybody's requirements.
>
> (Principal engineer)

Hence the emphasis on the personal relationship: 'we are so reliant on their technology that we have to keep close tabs on what they're doing and be aware of the next generation and we try to catch a lead on the competition by using them earlier' (principal engineer). Face to face contact was seen as vital for good relationships and the ability to ask suppliers for favours or special treatment from time to time: 'it is almost not on a business basis really, you get to know people, you do them favours, and they do you favours' (chief mechanical engineer).

Whatever the advantages of increasing interdependence, there were also real disadvantages. The major problem was the loss of distinctiveness of the product. Competitors had the same devices and, if these were important to the performance of the drive, then any technical originality disappeared. Yet it was too costly and inefficient to compete with specialist suppliers if there was little or no gain in performance. If managers lack the skill to identify the areas of design which should remain internally controlled, then an unsaleable product is likely to be the result. The global nature of the industry and its concentration in the USA and the Far East left Midas isolated from immediate contact with vendors, compounding the difficulties of working closely with them. Such suppliers generally had limited local resources and local representatives sometimes merely added to the problems of working with engineers in another continent by inserting one more filter in the communication chain. Engineers and managers spent considerable time in long distance conference calls at unsocial hours, or long distance travel. Relative isolation and distance may result in new technologies being missed until they are on the market. US companies for example often have no tie-up to the UK, with its limited disk-drive industry. Consequently, 'the sales engineers over here don't really know anything about disk drives so they don't get the information and if they get it they ignore it or they don't pass it on' (senior engineer). There is also a risk that local representatives of a distant supplier will over-promise, resulting in a market failure rather than stealing a march on the competition. Promises are more difficult to assess when casual, routine contact with vendor engineers is impossible because they are across the Atlantic:

> A lot of people will say they can make a certain device and they'll tell you they're going to be available in six months, but you can't really afford to base a whole drive on the promise that they can produce a chip in six months. . . . None of these things come out without bugs either . . . there is always something you have to get round. . . . It is always difficult getting that information which is one problem of being on this side of the Atlantic . . . a lot of these companies are American. . . . You're not on a face to face basis. . . . Getting information on the phone . . . and actually getting them to tell you what is wrong with a chip is quite . . . I mean, you know there are problems but getting them to find that information is difficult.
>
> (Senior engineer)

It was in the context of this recessionary, highly competitive and unstable industry that a new Midas management team had to restructure and reorient the firm. Much of the design and development team remained intact, with its history of phenomenal success as well as the immediate recollections of dramatic failure. The new vice president of engineering was a young man, originally a graduate member of the team and highly respected for his technical skills. The new chairman, and new directors, or vice presidents as they became, had the onerous task of recreating a viable business.

The total quality strategy and product development

The recovery strategy publicly recognised the impossibility of 'doing it all': the technology had moved on, the necessary expertise had become more differentiated and the 'kitchen table top mentality' could no longer compete with automated manufacturing facilities in the Far East. It was acknowledged that attempted autonomy had resulted in a lack of continuous development of technical expertise; inadequate external influence and control; technical roots in the era when the company began; and a tradition of engineers seeking to be 'indispensable lone rangers and prima donnas' (vice president of engineering). As discussed in Chapter 3, the new management team sought the participation of customers and suppliers in its business strategy. One important aspect of the total quality management rhetoric concerned the collaborative approach to expertise. At the time of our research, collaboration between the US and UK design teams was meant to provide a new synergy for product development, negotiations were under way to establish a joint manufacturing venture with a Japanese firm for a high volume product designed in the USA, and strategic partnerships with high-tech components' suppliers were being discussed. Tight timetables and the relative shortage of internal expertise in fact put a premium on collaboration. It was of course the role of management to ensure that this approach to development worked. We assess below the realities of attempted collaboration and discuss the failure of management to create a structure to facilitate effective innovation.

The central problem faced by the development group was the design of a technically feasible, innovatory, cost-controlled device according to a very tight timetable. The resolution of problems in development was thus central to future success. At the time of our research, morale was very low and anxiety about the future running high. Labour turnover was increasing, and the relative shortage of internal expertise continually threatened the timetable. Despite the increasing complexity of electronics on the drive itself and the pace of technical change in the industry, design and development work continued to focus on the short term, with whatever long-range R&D had been planned being continually postponed because of perceived market pressures. New strategies had not superseded this tradition. Both managers and engineers were obsessed with timescales. From the management perspective, the deadlines were difficult but inevitable. Time was money: any delay equalled loss of sales and a more expensive device. For the engineers the requirements of innovation were in conflict with rigid, management-imposed deadlines. They saw the tight timetable as counter-productive, with extreme time pressures increasing the rate of unnecessary technical errors and making collaboration with supplier engineers more and more fraught:

It all comes down to time. It is to cut corners, save time at the end of the day . . . Well the lead time on some of the parts . . . it's fourteen weeks, so you have three months to get prototypes. If we decide yes these are (for example the heads) we want, fourteen weeks later we get some samples in, we do an evaluation on them and decide we want some more. Another two to three months to wait. . . . So there's six months into schedule and after three months we're supposed to have a prototype drive. Everybody knows it's going to take two to three months to do the heads. . . . It's one of the standard things. And doing ASIC's as well. . . . So that is all predefined. But all they do is look at the end date, subtract that amount and say, well, you've got four weeks to design it. . . . It puts you under so much pressure.

(Principal engineer)

The vice president of engineering, let's call him Nick, having previously been development manager, felt well qualified to pronounce on the internal problems. His analysis was that the engineers lacked motivation and commitment. His prescription for recovery, however, centred on bringing them into line by wielding a metaphorical big stick. He espoused the merits of aggressive management, described by himself as the 'Attila the Hun' approach. With this in mind he had selected a new development manager, whom we will call Dennis, partly because of his perceived aggressive qualities and hence similarity to himself. Not surprisingly he provided Dennis with his analysis of the problem, giving him a thumbnail sketch of each engineer, which seemed to concentrate more on their deficiencies than on their merits. This made it difficult for the manager to adopt an independent stance. In Nick's view the company treated the engineers well, with good pay and promotion prospects, but they were ungrateful, responding only with yet more unreasonable demands and less effort. He had come to regard them as children needing a strong father figure to bring them into line and referred to the team as 'the kindergarten'. (In fact, both Nick and Dennis were younger than the senior engineers.) From management's perspective the complaints of the engineers could be set aside until after the next project deadline. Behind the 'time pressure' rationale lay another which emphasised the supposed pettiness of the engineers, refusing to set aside their grievances in the interests of the firm's survival. Nick drew unfavourable comparisons between the UK and the US development engineers, depicting the latter as endlessly willing and enthusiastic, in contrast with the 'we the union' approach of the UK group. The management response to any disaffection expressed by the engineers was not to seek improvement through more collaborative project management, but to adopt an increasingly directive, authoritarian stance, deepening the motivational crisis yet further:

It's all geared up for what the company can get from the individual. There's no sort of 'what can the company do for you' sort of thing. It's just all work, work, work and no play; pressure, pressure, pressure.

(Design engineer)

What I don't like is continually being expected, week after week, to work late at nights. I've got young kids and I like to get a chance to see them before they go to their beds. I don't mind doing the hours but I don't like continuous hours. There's never any light at the end of the tunnel. That's another reason why I'm leaving.

(Project leader)

We have spoken to the MD a couple of times and he has asked what the problems were . . . why we weren't all on cloud nine and fired up raring to go and somebody stood up and started telling him what the problems were and he was effectively shot down. Now if you have management with that attitude, why do they ask if they're not interested. . . . You think, well, why should we bother?

(Senior design engineer)

Dennis was in fact installed in his post with at least two contradictory agendas. Not only was he under pressure from Nick to establish his authority over the senior engineers, who were depicted as the main trouble makers, he was also expected to introduce a higher standard of progressive management, focusing on the development of expertise. He was meant to use his prior experience in TE, the US multinational widely respected for its 'human resources' style of management, to provide a model of good practice. He was not intended to have a direct technical role; indeed, his own engineering background was in a different specialism. His first public statements raised hopes among the younger engineers of a new participatory, egalitarian management. He was not welcomed by the more senior engineers, however, who were willing to express publicly their doubts about what precisely he was able to contribute. For many of the engineers, his subsequent actions opened up a gulf between the new espoused organic structure and the reality of a mechanistic, punitive style of control.

He began by eradicating the old departmental structure, where senior engineers had relative autonomy in project management. Everyone reported direct to him, regardless of technical specialism or status. From the management point of view, the senior engineers could no longer be trusted in such roles because of failure to meet past deadlines. The engineers, in contrast, argued that they could not accept responsibility for a development timetable which was, in their professional judgement, impossible to meet. The conventional project management role thus became diluted and contentious. The flat structure was presented as an interim arrangement, while a new structure, intended to incorporate some of Dennis's own appointments in key roles, was devised. His professed intention was to devise a matrix structure with project planning on one axis and expertise along the other. The expertise axis was intended to give senior engineers control over their disciplinary groups, facilitating on-the-job training and career progression. Newly appointed programme managers would form the other axis. These would co-ordinate technical experts and manage the perceived conflict between technical excellence and commercial success, but would not have formal authority over the senior engineers. Reporting responsibilities would still converge on the development manager. These changes were not greeted with enthusiasm: Dennis's motives were suspected and the engineers resisted the division between project management and technical expertise, which was interpreted as a way of excluding them from both project planning and the higher paid management roles. Lacking the consent of the senior engineers, his attempts to control the development timetable became less and less feasible. The relationships between manager and engineers deteriorated, damaging technical progress and undermining changes towards more organic management.

The role of development manager quickly became distorted: instead of concentrating on the development of expertise, and creating a reasoned balance between external and internal inputs, recruiting new engineers in areas of perceived weakness and ensuring that corporate resources were directed accordingly, Dennis became more and more involved in the day to day project management role for which he was poorly qualified. He was perceived to be failing to maintain a commitment to regular performance appraisal and feedback. There was a felt absence of clear lines of reporting, with many engineers uncertain whether they should report to their immediate superior in their specialism or direct to the manager. Supposed career structures were regarded with a high degree of cynicism. Lack of a clear reporting structure led to jealousies and resentments at perceived favouritism. As far as the engineers were concerned, the bases of reward and recognition were not only implicit, but also applied arbitrarily. Everyone felt the shortage of internal expertise, and although recruitment was meant to be a priority, in practice it was frequently postponed in favour of a more pressing technical crisis in the current project: 'we are very short staffed, there is no slack in the timetable . . . as soon as something goes wrong the whole pack of cards is going to fall down' (senior engineer). New recruitment at junior levels would have eased the pressures, but no one wanted to train such recruits. Moreover the distrust between Dennis and the engineers resulted in proposed recruitment at senior levels being seen as damaging career prospects for the middle ranks. Midas's declining reputation added one more strand of difficulty: there was continuing hesitation about open advertising of vacancies and a tacit fear that no one would want to work for them if they knew beforehand the history of the company. Recruitment tended to be contracted out to private agencies who matched engineers on their files with Midas requirements. The balance between in-house and external expertise was thus an *ad hoc* affair, dominated by short-term considerations and limiting the development of a consistent policy on the use of external expertise.

Dennis badly needed the respect of the engineers in order to move the existing design projects forward. He lacked the obvious basis for such respect, because he had no experience as a disk-drive engineer. Increasingly anxious to demonstrate that he could 'get stuck in' and help out with technical problems, he tried to assert his technical prowess, a tactic which was viewed sceptically by the engineers who disliked the feeling of having someone trying to do their jobs. Dennis was not unaware of their attitude: 'It's "Here he comes again with his idiot questions" ' (manager). The engineers complained of the 'twenty questions style of management' and felt he should not be looking over their shoulders but should be developing a better management structure: 'We shouldn't need to pay him so much to debug boards' (engineers). He was personally undermined and further handicapped in carrying out the developmental role he was recruited for. He felt himself excluded from the more exciting aspects of the work: 'Nick and other people in the company who were previously designing (the product) have a different level of interaction sometimes, which excludes me . . .'. His own boss, he felt, did not trust him to manage the group: 'what he does is continue as if I wasn't there. . . . He's gone in and done, he has really hijacked what I really should be doing. . . . And that leaves me to wonder how I can continue at times, to be honest' (manager). The role was probably an impossible one to fulfil: he was 'the meat in the sandwich' between corporate management and the engineers. Dennis felt that his boss wanted to make him into his instrument or mouthpiece, 'an image of him', and that his own lack of specialist expertise was used against him, giving Nick an excuse to 'wade in' at any time and usurp whatever fragile authority he had established. Despite attempts at resistance he was caught in the contradiction between the control directives from above and the need to gain the acceptance of the engineers.

In the face of continuing distrust, and with the objective of meeting deadlines, Nick and Dennis imposed a system of direct control which appeared to have a short-term instrumental rationality. Dennis tacitly became programme manager for both new and existing projects. He then tried to set up routine, frequent project meetings to chase progress and to specify a highly detailed division of labour for each stage of the timetable.

Timesheets were introduced in conjunction with daily work plans, which were meant to feed in to annual performance appraisals. Nick in turn expected progress reports on every facet of the projects at daily intervals. The engineers regarded such minute supervision, and the reporting work which it produced, as a distraction from the 'real work' of design. As far as they were concerned, Dennis had fallen back on a form of mechanistic control, relying on his formal status and 'disenfranchising' them from the planning process. The more the engineers were felt to be resisting, however, the more Dennis and Nick 'punished' them by seeking to impose yet more reporting requirements and by further exclusion from project planning. Although experiencing enormous work pressure, the engineers felt that the time allocated to design work was being reduced. The more the management structure emphasised the separation of the planning from the execution of product development, the more instrumental and defensive the engineers became. Given the intangible character of much of the work, the system of direct control was largely counter-productive. This was especially true in the context of little respect for the 'planner' by those expected to 'do': 'they don't trust me to make decisions which would allow us to proceed and succeed' (Dennis).

Thus the espoused organic style of management never transpired. Instead informal, historically based norms continued to dominate actual practice. The relatively authoritarian tradition remained the common approach to dealing with mistakes and failures. If there was a management ethos it was about finding a scapegoat: 'it was always "who's to blame for this or that", never "OK that's wrong, let's fix it" ' (senior engineer).

Effects on formal and informal dimensions of supplier relationships

Vendor management has become one of the catch phrases of the 1980s and 1990s. Partnership talk had permeated both the development and the purchasing function at Midas: developing strong, integrated relationships with strategic suppliers was espoused as a key to quality and cost control of inventory. Much emphasis was placed on the need to develop good personal relationships, with a degree of continuity, and to be directive about specifying the requirements on both sides. This means, in the jargon, a hands-on approach to the other's business if necessary. It also assumes that there are mutual gains to be made from this style of doing business.

The reality of 'partnership' was rather different for Midas, however, with declining market power and limited ability to generate responsiveness from its suppliers. Customers struggling with cash flow are treated less favourably by vendors, who are themselves prioritising orders from the prompt payers. Increasing interdependence tied Midas in to suppliers' timetables outside its control. Such suppliers were well aware of the threat potential which they held for Midas schedules: 'the problem is next week will do for them and yesterday will do for us' (design engineer). Not surprisingly, distrust within the design team made already tense relationships with suppliers even more difficult.

The relative exclusion of the engineers from project planning meant that management-defined changes to the design specification were regarded as negating any technical progress which had been made and as undermining trust between the engineers and their contacts in suppliers. Regular alterations to the specification resulted in suppliers being expected to take on further simulation and prototype work, before any payment was forthcoming. The PCB for each new device for example was subcontracted to a specialist supplier. The PCB is an intricate part of the design: certain parameters are fixed by mechanical specifications of the drive, but over and above this the designer has to find, from a seemingly infinite variety of routes, the most efficient solution to linking all the required components into a workable circuit. Described by Dennis as the 'tail wagged by the dog', the PCB engineer is dependent on all the other engineers completing their aspect of the design before the PCB specification can be fixed and schematics sent off for prototyping. Timetable pressures and attempts to take short cuts in the electronics were resulting in continual redesign of the PCB. By the time the PCB layout had been formalised, the design specification had changed:

> It's not development – 'right we have got something, send it off, get it back, check it, that's it – it's always 'we'll send it off before it's ready, and we'll do some development in the meantime, and then we'll change it . . .'. They must waste more time checking five of these art works than getting them right in the first place.
>
> (Design engineer)

The perceived lack of time also meant that, despite the total quality rhetoric, the relationship between the purchasing function and development remained much as it had always been. Total quality techniques and vendor management put a premium on a purchasing group with considerable engineering skills and the time and resources to work with key vendors. Midas in fact had a very limited, and traditional, reactive purchasing function, relying heavily on one manager with responsibility for controlling all inventory. Within the development group the need to work with vendor engineers had resulted in many professional partnerships, underlined by friendships, established over a number of years. No doubt such friendships were not straightforward because of their commercial origins. Loyalties to peers, as opposed to the firm, are tested when technical developments, competition and a degree of professional rivalry underlie the relationship. Nevertheless, such exchanges do have a genuinely collaborative dimension: both buyers and suppliers want to know what advances are being made in their respective technical areas. Without access to the informal networks, the products on both sides would be less successful.

At the commercial level, represented by the purchasing function, although partnership was the dominant rhetoric, it was clear that short-term cost control was the priority. The manager saw her role as the reduction of uncertainty in the costing and supply of appropriate materials and components. Hard bargaining, focused on direct and indirect costs, formed the main substance of supplier relationships. Most of her efforts in fact centred on agreeing prices and lead times for the high-value components. With such key vendors she would be in day to day contact with commercial representatives, because 'the inventory management of these parts basically controls the cash flow of the company' (purchasing manager). During Midas's successful period,

> You could almost tell suppliers what they had to supply you. It was very simple. The value we spend ... it gives you a very high profile. ... Similarly when the company ran out of money, those vendors [who are solely suppliers to the disk-drive manufacturers] were at the highest exposure and those were the vendors you had to work hardest with to try and get production moving.
>
> (Purchasing manager)

The news of Midas's 1989 collapse had been devastating for some suppliers and co-operative business with these had become correspondingly more difficult. The closure of operations, and the refinancing arrangements, had left a debt to vendors of US$17 million. The purchasing manager had faced the unenviable task of persuading them to give further credit. Many suppliers, having grown originally with Midas, supported the firm: 'it is ever so humbling really, because these people kept us afloat, basically'. Many of these companies were themselves in financial straits, and in some cases needed Midas to remain in operation to provide part of their market. Most creditors, approached individually to reschedule payment over a longer period, agreed to new terms, together with cash on delivery for further orders. They had little choice perhaps but to minimise potential damage to their own business. Hard bargaining by the purchasing manager also gained an average 15 per cent price reduction from suppliers. This had not made the manager popular: in classic 'blame the messenger' style, and no doubt because of her gender, she had achieved a degree of notoriety for her negotiating skills, and was labelled by some vendors as 'the black witch of the north'.

The difficulties did not end with the re-establishing of supply relationships. The hardest negotiations continued to be those where the company was committed to using a particular supplier: 'basically they have the clout and you are virtually led by the hand' (purchasing manager). In these cases, her strategy was highly proactive, with constant search for alternative, cheaper developments from competing firms. Meanwhile any incentive available was used to clinch a deal: the promise of long-term orders, flexibility about delivery of goods, agreeing to a stock level to suit the supplier's financial year, account management devices and so on. At this level, whatever the rhetoric, and however good the informal engineering contacts, the reality was institutionalised suspicion and the tactics of hard distributive bargaining.

The bargaining surrounding the specification and acquisition of a high-value component of the drive, the heads and disks assembly, illustrates the interplay between the formal and the informal levels of vendor management in a particularly acute form. Midas was dependent on a US supplier, ABC, for the assembly. In the old days Midas had been a favoured customer (there were stories of the days when the Midas managing director could turn up at the supplier's factories in the Far East to 'expedite production') but, at the time of our study, relationships had soured: 'we have a vendor who is really acting the pig, but basically will sour the relationship. What we have to do is find out what is this guy's problem. Our problem is we are too reliant on him . . . ' (purchasing manager). Midas was deeply in debt to ABC, and now appeared to be expecting further credit. ABC was itself facing financial problems and widely believed to be deciding who to work for first, on the basis of who was most likely to pay quickest. Midas had no threat potential open to them because they were aware that other customers would willingly take over any cancelled time in ABC's pro- duction schedules, potentially paying a higher price for similar goods. The supplier threatened to renege on the contract or to let the forecast lead time slip by evasiveness and prevarication. At this point, senior management were drafted in to try to avert disaster with whatever promises of payment and further business they were able to make. The accurate specification of minimum performance requirements by the designer is essential to the per- formance of the finished product. The specification has to be completed early in the timetable, because lead times for the assembly are considerable, typically twelve to fourteen weeks, out of a timetable of six or seven months. Errors in specification have thus become increasingly critical. In the past there had been time to experiment with alternative prototypes, encouraging considerable informal exchange between buyer and vendor engineers. Latterly computer simulation of the assembly had become the norm, with the emphasis on getting the heads and disks combination right first time. True to its past form, Midas had little in-house expertise in simulation of any part of the drive. Management continued to resist investment in the necessary software, which was regarded as expensive and unnecessary. The conventional practice was to rely on the expertise of the supplier to carry out simulation. If the product specification kept changing, however, Midas ran the risk of losing their place in the supplier's production schedule. Whereas an in-house capability would have allowed changes to the assembly to be modelled and evaluated on demand, dependence on the supplier could mean a wait of a week or longer, and yet more lost time.

The engineer responsible for specifying the assembly had a long-standing, close relationship with his peers in the USA. He talked to them on the phone most days and spent considerable work time involved directly or indirectly in negotiating the technical specification. He visited a number of times a year and enjoyed the high social life which was the norm on such occasions. Aware of the worsening relationship between the two companies, and of his loss of credibility internally if he failed to get the assembly in time to slot into the development timetable, he tried to use the bait of a technically interesting challenge to persuade ABC engineers to carry on working for him, as opposed to other customers. At the end of the day, the declining market power of Midas outweighed technical challenge and friendship: 'what hap- pened today is they just don't want to know' (design engineer). His key contact at research engineer level was under pressure to work for bigger customers: 'a difficult and at times embarrassing position to be in' (design engineer). Here the micro-politics of internal relationships in engineering are also relevant. The engineer, with a Ph.D. in superconductivity resented the lack of opportunity to do research on the drive, feeling himself to be instead a 'technician' responsible for negotiating with vendors who did all the research elsewhere. His skills were doubted by Nick, however, who regarded him as too vague to produce an accurate specification of the assembly. The engineer wanted to persuade Nick to buy in modelling software so that he could engage directly in a higher level technical dialogue with his ABC peers. His boss was resistant, and thought that the engineer should 'prove himself' first with-out the aid of modelling tools. This lack of trust internally adversely affected the engineer's control over external expertise and, along with the deterior-ating institutional relationship between the firms, contributed to yet more delay.

Failed attempts at collaboration: internal supplier relationships or 'them and us' in product development and the failure to incorporate new technology

> It's a bit of a them and us type thing. They seem to get everything they want and we can't get any equipment.
>
> (Design engineer)

If the main engineering area was meant to be here, which is what we have been told on several occasions, then why is the VP of engineering in the US? . . . Well the natural assumption is that he wants engineering based where he is. And that worries a lot of people in here. So people are a bit edgy about the future.

(Design engineer)

Product development was split into two areas. In theory, the US team was working on a high-volume, low-cost product for the personal computer market, while the more established UK team was responsible for the high-value workstation market. In practice the two teams appeared to be divided not only by product area and the Atlantic but also by mutual suspicion. For the UK group, the relative inaccessibility of the US team, and Nick's perceived favouritism towards them, exacerbated the feelings of doubt about the real agenda for future development. The teams were meant to be collaborating, sharing intellectual and financial resources in the development of products. In practice there was little sharing of knowledge and the UK group acted as though they were in competition both for technical resources in the short term and their own jobs in the future:

The few engineers [in the US team] I have dealings with are very reluctant to pass on any information at all. In fact on one occasion that I tried to get some information, not information that was going to be used as a weapon or anything like that, I had to answer a series of questions before he would deliver. . . . I had to remind him that we were working for the same company.

(Project leader)

Engineers in the UK group bemoaned the fact that the others appeared to get the software tools that they needed to carry out their projects, while being able to exercise an informal veto on resource requests from the British group. Why else should requests for tools vital to the current design be the subject of long delays, while target dates slipped further behind?

Suspicion and rivalries between the groups contributed to the failure to innovate in the newest design project. Work was in progress on both sides of the Atlantic to replace analogue techniques with digital signal processing (DSP). DSP has the advantage of creating a more intelligent and higher performing product. The US group was further advanced, but an experienced engineer was hired specifically to develop the appropriate model for the UK project. The DSP work for the new drive was delayed because he lacked access to the software tools necessary for what-if mathematical modelling. The deadline for engineering prototypes continued to approach, while the two groups were caught in time consuming wrangles about the justification for purchase of the software and the appropriate workstation. The engineer responsible for work on DSP was sufficiently excited about the project to demand that the company sent him to the USA to work with his peers and to use their software tools. On arrival, little provision was made to incorporate him into the group and he found himself working alone. Despite working intensively on the design, by the time he returned to Britain the deadline for engineering samples had been used to force amendment, re-incorporating the old analogue system, despite its known problems, and excluding the use of DSP. To his dismay, he was reassigned to work on a technical problem left over from a previous project. Ironically, the simulation software was subsequently purchased but left to gather dust in the cupboard. The result was failure to incorporate new technology and loss of competitive edge for the product.

The consequences for product innovation

There is never enough time to do the job properly, but there is time enough to do it again and again and again.

(Design engineer)

In this context, technical expertise cannot be treated as simply a business resource to be bought in, or contracted out, and allocated to projects according to a rational plan. Distrust between senior management and the most established engineers, responsible for leading the design work, undermined the development of expertise and innovation. The engineers increasingly used their knowledge as a defensive weapon to protect their status and to protect themselves from a perceived threat of displacement, either by incoming programme managers or by contract labour.

The effect of attempts to impose direct control on the senior engineers was to make them feel diminished in status: 'You're not really allowed to manage, you're just a scapegoat' (senior engineer); 'it's almost like being back at school. . . . I've always had a reasonable amount of responsibility in this place. I still do, but it's just the way you get treated now . . . you've got to ask permission to do everything. It's like there is a lack of trust' (principal engineer). Their resentment against their perceived loss of dignity made them increasingly instrumental and highly resistant to accepting technical responsibility without real authority. The more established engineers were consequently protective and exclusive about their expertise. They sought to control access to knowledge about development techniques in their specialist areas. There was an implicit refusal to delegate the creative aspects of design or to train incomers in the skills of the trade. The junior engineers experienced this as *laissez-faire* management. No one appeared to care whether they did their job or not, and there were no clear guidelines on what should be done: 'there seems to be a band in here, a group of engineers who go away and decide things and that's it and you never hear anything more. If management can improve that, and start telling people "we need this, you do it", ... instead they say "we need this done, do it if you want" ' (ex-engineer). Junior engineers, recruited for a specific area of expertise, found themselves diverted onto routine product engineering, left in a corner, or at worst given problems they were unqualified to solve and then blamed for their incompetence. They became disenchanted, if not deeply hurt, and eventually resigned, creating further shortage of labour.

A clear example of such mismanagement occurred in relation to the development of what was intended to be a low-cost product designed to help the company's cash flow. At the time of our research, the product was very late and still hampered by technical problems. With the objective of saving money, a decision had been taken to design a control device internally, instead of buying it in as had been done in the past. This had proved to be a costly 'saving' at both technical and personal levels. First the technical difficulty had been underestimated; no one appeared able or willing to create an effective solution, resulting in an inadequate device which was fixed up by adding on extra, expensive, components: 'it works at the moment but only because we are doing a lot of not exactly ethical things to the electronics. I mean sticking on bits here and there that shouldn't really need to be there. So component costs have gone up' (junior engineer). The product was no longer cost-cutting and the most optimistic view was that in production it might break even, if any customers could be found. Second the recently recruited graduate quoted above, who was landed with the problem, became the last of a series of scapegoats and left the company, his confidence undermined, after being blamed for incompetence. In a sequence of events which seemed to be repeated with each recent recruit, he was selected for his skills in software development but was instead assigned to solve the motor control problem after senior engineers abandoned it. He was not warned about its history and was moreover unqualified technically. None of the senior engineers came to his assistance, and he became discouraged, but did not take action on his own behalf. The manager who recruited him had left the company and he was unsure of who to speak to. His appearance and reliability deteriorated, and this seemed to be viewed as an indicator of technical incompetence. Eventually he was given a very negative performance review by Dennis, who gave him a two month probation period in which to improve, and a new task in an area relevant to his skills. After two months, however, nothing happened: no further feedback, positive or negative, was forthcoming. The manager had moved on to the latest crisis. The engineer remained extremely agitated and resigned a few weeks later.

The defensiveness of the senior engineers was particularly damaging to any attempt to build continuous improvements into the design cycle. Existing knowledge was not routinely incorporated into new projects and new expertise remained unused. In fact, there was evidence that design mistakes went uncorrected from one generation of products to the next:

> Someone comes up with an initial design. You get it onto the board, you find all the problems. The initial designer leaves the project and goes onto something else, and then it's us, the junior engineers, left to tackle the problem and try and fix it. Again that brings resentment. You know, 'I'm always left with the rubbish, someone else gets the new design'. They'll probably make the same mistakes over and over again and I'll have to keep fixing the same mistakes over and over again. It's a very vicious circle.
>
> (Design engineer)

The senior engineers regarded an ability to 'work round the problems' as the trademark of a true expert. From the perspective of the junior engineers, the 'learning by doing' approach of the established engineers could be improved, but was not open to discussion. Hence they felt the lack of any opportunity to feed in formal knowledge, acquired from university or programming courses, or conversely to benefit from the acquired experience of the design team:

> I was talking to Robert who had been told to ask me why I was leaving and I just said 'I am losing my edge'. They don't seem to want to involve the younger engineers . . . they don't ask for input from you.
>
> (Design engineer)

The result was that traditional 'always done it this way' approaches went unchallenged, and known technical problems and potential solutions were reinvented with each new product:

> What surprised me was that it's a known problem that this technique produces a lot of electrical noise . . . which seems to have been totally forgotten. I didn't realise that until well into the time I was working on this thing. I was talking to them and 'oh, we knew this, we knew we had this problem when we worked on the 8 inch version'. So I am annoyed that that got through because it is a known problem. . . . It's like knowledge in this place is kept in the designer's head, there is no real written documentation. . . . The time to correct it now, well it has been too little too late . . . there seems to be a severe problem in communication of knowledge. . . . That was one of the things (the manager) tried to blame me for during my review. He had written down severe lack of docu-

mentation and I pointed out to him that I was actually doing some documentation and was told to stop doing it, stop wasting time. . . .
(Junior engineer, working on the motor control problem described above)

Middle rank engineers also experienced themselves as excluded from participation in design work and resented having to clear up the mess left by the design originators, who had moved on to the next project. Errors designed into the last product were not corrected and scarce engineering resources were devoted to clearing up the same mistakes again and again:

There seems to be a group of people who are involved in the next generation of products. That may consist of five or six people. But they don't make the major decisions. And there is the rest of engineering which are called the 'shit shovellers' who come along behind them and have to make it work. And meanwhile they have moved on to the next product, and are creating the next disaster. And these people that come along behind never get a chance to input into the design cycle in the early days.

(Engineer)

Thus the majority of the group, although working in the same, open plan office every day, were excluded from decisions about the design parameters. Their experience gained as a result of 'cleaning up after the last mess' was lost, or their skills unused, and constructive criticism became personal bitterness.

All of these dynamics were visibly at work in relation to the major innovative development taking place during our fieldwork. The design timetable for the new project was set for six months, but no one seemed to be able to get started. During Nick's visits to the team, he talked ominously about needing 'an event' to signify the start: a sacking or a death, perhaps. The timetable immediately slipped by two months, mainly due to external suppliers' lead times and the inability of Midas senior managers to apply pressure on key suppliers. As competitors released technical specifications for their own new products, the internal design specification continued to change throughout the summer of 1990. The intended release date seemed set to slip further into spring 1991, but was reset for December, as a result of a management decision to revert to using some aspects of the old design, despite its known problems. By August 1990 the revised schedule was also slipping, and engineers continued to be diverted onto production problems with existing products. Dennis put pressure on the engineers to work increasingly long hours and weekends and resented the incursion of holidays. At an August meeting to finalise the specification, it was agreed that finished engineering samples should be tested by February 1991, with production set for June/July. In fact by August 1991 the test and evaluation procedures had still not begun. A year before, optimistic expectations of being able to match the production schedules of potential customers were expressed at the meetings between development, marketing and production. The marketing manager predicted steady profit from the forecast product market. By August 1991, the device was at least six months off production and the company was in receivership.

Conclusion: how to get it wrong

> It made me wonder how a company that had been in the industry so long, with so much good engineering experience, how they could manage to get it so drastically wrong. It's just a disaster.
>
> (Ex-design engineer)

Governments, business schools and management textbooks stress the positive organisational consequences of adapting to the market. But it is the way of things that disasters are often more instructive than successes. For Midas management the 'discipline of the market' resulted not in effective innovation, but in fear of failure, and inability to develop appropriate structures for the management of internal and external expertise. Ironically, senior managers' pursuit of a short-term instrumental rationality for development undermined the achievement of their own objectives and produced a damaging pattern of distrust and defensiveness within engineering. The result was a motivational crisis among the engineers, the collapse of management legitimacy and loss of control over the development process, all of which contributed to the failure of the business.

Midas senior managers espoused the virtues of total quality techniques and an organic, human resources style of operation, but acted according to a short-term, instrumental rationality. The apparent logic of mechanistic control, punitive deadlines and aggressive tactics, however, lead not to speedy, efficient work, innovative designs and a reasoned balance between external and internal sources of expertise, but to expensive mistakes and further delays. As management attempted to shift the balance of power over technical innovation in their favour, the gap between engineers' expectations of technical control and the reality of technical accountability without power created the conditions for intensified low trust. For expert groups, when the expectation of relative autonomy and egalitarian management breaks down, a motivational crisis and poor performance are likely to be the result. In this case, 'open management' was an excuse for lack of delegation and consistent routines which should have provided the basis for innovation. The contradiction experienced between the espoused and the actual practice of management resulted in a damaging pattern of workplace relations, which might be characterised (in a parody of the infamous 'Four Ps' of marketing textbooks) as the 'Four Ds' of Distrust, Divisiveness, Defensiveness and Doubt about the future of the company. Once the dynamics of the Four Ds are in place, they are likely to result, particularly in periods of economic recession, in failure to manage innovation, despite reasonable technical resources and access to expertise. Or, to put it in the format of the trite little aphorism so characteristic of the airport management textbook, 4D + 1D = 5D: Distrust + Divisiveness + Defensiveness + Doubt = Disaster!

Regardless of good intentions to reform past practices, senior managers proved unable to create a structure to control timetables and costs, while enabling innovative design and development work to proceed. As in Burns and Stalker's work, the ability of the directors and senior management of the company to interpret the requirements of the situation and to take appropriate action is highlighted. In this case the central dilemma concerned the perceived conflict between technical excellence and commercial success. Fear of failure amongst top management resulted in a pattern of defensive avoidance. Management actions focused increasingly on the control of costs and the timetable, to the exclusion of other, more subtle, considerations. Controlling these tangible variables seemed to promise an effective way forward. Ironically, the very measures taken to exert control resulted in further inefficiency and high social costs, including the loss of significant numbers of jobs. For the managers, fearful that an alternative strategy giving greater control to the engineers would not result in commercial success, defensive avoidance resulted in loss of their credibility and eventually loss of their own jobs.

The events at Midas are forceful reminders of the fallibility of real managers, as opposed to their depiction in many prescriptive texts as either omnipotent beings dispassionately implementing policy without opposition or technocrats whose conduct is determined by structural imperatives. Management control systems are often internally contradictory and unstable, reflecting the practical dilemmas of innovation, production and marketing. The prescription of open management and collaborative development, initiated and controlled from the top, and introduced with purely instrumental motives, does not easily overcome a history of punitive management and deep-seated belief in the right of management to manage without having their authority questioned. It is unlikely to provide an easy solution to problems of poor performance and does not guarantee the commitment of technical experts to the goals of senior management. In this case attempts to create a more organic structure were fraught with contradiction and personally costly because they threatened existing patterns of authority within management, and engineering, career hierarchies. For many small and medium-sized engineering firms, locked into a highly competitive and unstable supply chain, the experience of Midas engineers and managers represents a potentially common crisis: the growing contradiction between espoused collaborative development and total quality management and the reality of anxious bargaining with supposed strategic partners, intensification of work, increased monitoring and control, and demands for results yesterday (Webb 1992).

6 The user–supplier relationship

USERS AND SUPPLIERS IN CONTEXT

Those problems and dilemmas of expert management inside the firm, explored in the previous two chapters, are only half the story. In the high-technology marketplaces of the computer systems sector, supply chain relationships, and the balance between internal and external sources of expertise, are critical to success. In reality, the single loop binding a customer and a supplier is made up of two sub-relationships, user–supplier and supplier–user. However simple or complex the technology, the transactions take place in a very competitive marketplace, against an unstable backdrop of rapid innovation, takeovers and constant manoeuvring for competitive advantage by both suppliers and users. The highly charged economic environment is a dangerous habitat for the manager, concerned as ever with the reduction of uncertainty. The very instability of the marketplace offers great rewards to those who get it right, but also holds out the constant possibility of failure. To managers in both suppliers and customers, controlling the supply chain is an important means of controlling the risks of participation in an inherently unpredictable market.

The problem for managers – and for the analysis of managerial actions – is that there are a number of different ways to control such relationships. These strategies have the same end – maximising profit – but can have diametrically opposed means. In some contexts, where there are alternative sources of supply and the customer is powerful enough to dictate the terms of the relationship, senior managers may manage suppliers aggressively, playing one off against the other and accepting the frequent confrontations that go with the strategy. Others may follow less opportunistic, more long-term strategies, attempting to construct stable relationships with suppliers. A third firm might attempt to steer a middle course, reserving collaborative strategies for technologies it defines as centrally important, but following a more confrontational line for technologies it regards as peripheral.

It would be comforting to think that research could reveal some clear-cut relationships between particular approaches to the management of supply chain relationships and important market variables. It would be nice to know, for example, that confrontational approaches go with markets characterised by high levels of innovation. The real world, unfortunately, is messier than that: no sooner does research seem to point to a conclusion in one area than generalisations are undermined by contrasting findings elsewhere. One reason for this is that user–supplier relationships exist at several different levels simultaneously. To a social scientist, it goes without saying that any commercial transaction that is not a spot contract (the purchase of a small fixed-price item, like buying a can of baked beans in a supermarket) will have a social dimension to it, wrapped around the economic kernel of the transaction like the shell of a nut. One result of this is contradiction: actions at different levels may diverge from, and even actively subvert, the motives proclaimed by actors. In many user–supplier relationships, confrontational strategies are followed at one level, most commonly over pricing, at the same time that technical staff in the user are ringing up their friends and colleagues in a supplier to ensure they have an inside track on a forthcoming tender. When we talk about supply chain relationships, it is important to remember that this is in the first instance a relationship between people who represent companies. When the whole complex of relationships between a user and a supplier is taken into account, it becomes clear that there are both formal and informal dimensions.

As preceding chapters have tried to make clear, we should not take the formal dimension of business enterprises – explicit company policies and the organisational structures designed to implement them – at face value. One approach to the management of supplier relations may be proclaimed by senior management, and even institutionalised in the form of specialist purchasing departments or full-time negotiators, but this does not mean that senior management's vision will be shared or implemented by the actors involved in dealing with suppliers at various organisational levels. When staff from users and suppliers meet to thrash out the detail of an economic transaction, they each attempt to convince the other that there are also non-financial costs and benefits to the deal. Sales representatives might argue the strategic advantages to the user of acquiring access to the expertise their company has in this and related technologies if they will only buy the Acme System X. Reputation, on both sides, is generally at stake. If a supplier can solve certain problems for the customer, that customer will generally add to the non-financial 'capital' of the supplier in the potential marketplace of other buyers. Conversely, suppliers can spread rumours to the effect that a buyer is a manipulative time-waster, and that the group of people in the buyer's firm who are meant to evaluate new systems are dedicated instead to justifying their own existence by absorbing the sales efforts of suppliers: 'we know they are going to spend forever basically prattling about and never getting anything done' (Telewave Electronics (TE) sales manager). On the other hand, users may worry that their experts in a highly specialised technology may be poached if they are allowed to work too closely with supplier experts.

Any analysis of supply chain relationships which attempts to engage with them as they are, and not as they are idealised or theorised by senior managers and business school courses, therefore has to deal with a tangled mess of mixed motives, formal and informal dimensions of business organisation, and a wide range of social actors. An adequate rendering of this level of complexity is often called 'thick description' by anthropologists (Geertz, 1973). It is fair to question whether the simple division of user–supplier relations into collaborative and confrontational approaches can be justified in 'thick descriptions' of business transactions. The first point to make is that the contrast between collaborative and confrontational approaches to the management of supplier relationships is discursive rather than real. In other words, the vocabulary used both by managers and management studies to describe action ('confrontational', 'collaborative', 'adversarial') is made up of idealised categories. In all but the most exceptional cases, we argue, the user–supplier relationship varies according to the level of the relationship examined. It is the case that when asked to talk about relationships with suppliers, managers classify them by locating them along a mental axis with confrontational at one end and collaborative at the other, and the axis means a great deal to those involved in constructing user–supplier relationships. When a senior manager calls a supplier relationship collaborative, the word can, however, cover a multitude of sins.

Similarly where there is institutionalised confrontation between users and suppliers at one level, there may also be informal co-operation at others, as friends, peers and technical experts on both sides find themselves unwilling to break a network of social ties and obligations for a supplier policy devised by senior managers, but only very rarely after consultation with middle management, let alone technical experts and the shopfloor. We have already seen, in the case of informal feedback loops, that when work relationships evolve into social ties, they acquire a life of their own and often become very resistant to pressure from companies or managements. Many employees will seek ways around policies which seek to change established supply chains, even as they pay lip-service to them.

All supply relationships can be thought of as political with a small p. They revolve around commercial transactions where there is a basic clash of interests – suppliers want as much revenue as they can make, users to pay as little as they can get away with. Such relationships are basically to do with power, about the ability of either user or supplier to gain advantage at the other's expense. This elementary fact is sometimes obscured beneath the rhetoric of co-operation among managers, which is often extended to describe the active supply chain management prescribed by organisational philosophies such as total quality management (TQM) and just-in-time (JIT). The balance of power between supplier and user depends on three interdependent variables: the nature of the technology being supplied, the nature of the marketplace where it is transacted, and the *balance of expertise* between user and supplier, a concept that was introduced in Chapter 2. Taken together, these three factors make up the parameters of the power struggle between users and suppliers, but it should be stressed that they are linked and interact with each other over time. For example, if we treat the computer industry in very general terms, we could explain its development over the last thirty years by saying that large and expensive mainframes, produced by a small number of big companies which were able to dominate the market for many years, meant that for a long period the balance of expertise was very much in favour of suppliers. However, as the market matured in the 1970s, increasing computing expertise among users combined with enormous demand to fuel the boom in personal computing which began in the late 1970s, the first step along the road to distributed computing, along which we are still travelling a decade later.

The result was that a number of highly innovatory suppliers, Apple being the mythic example, were able to challenge the older mainframe suppliers and radically alter the nature of the computing marketplace in the process. In the maturer markets of the 1990s, we find a more equitable balance of expertise between users and suppliers. The balance of power tends to oscillate with the pace of innovation as suppliers gain temporary advantages in new technologies until users become familiar with applications. In recent years especially, users have had the terms of trade altered in their favour by the nature of change in the marketplace, where the proliferation of niche suppliers has fragmented the market, giving users a much wider range of choices and raising the level of competition between suppliers to unprecedented heights. To understand the user–supplier relationship, therefore, we need to look in some detail at the variables which determine the balance of power between them.

The nature of the technology

Particular technologies in the computer systems sector may have structural features that bear directly on the user–supplier relationship. The most notorious are the proprietary operating systems that attempt to lock users into a particular hardware supplier. However, with the continuing negotiations between major suppliers on open systems of one form or another, it seems that proprietary operating systems will be much less important in the future than they have been in the past. More relevant to the concerns of this chapter is what could be called the internal architecture of a computer system. Some technologies, like an automatic process control system (APCS), can be extended almost indefinitely without altering the internal architecture. This means, for example, that an APCS is essentially the same system in a small distillery as in a large oil refinery: the only difference is the number of input–ouput loops needed to cope with the larger number of monitoring and control points in the refinery, and these are simply added onto the system without altering its basic architecture. If a user wished, it would be possible to acquire an APCS from one supplier and later have it extended by another. The technology of digitalised process control does not vary in its essentials between suppliers, and any of the single-figure number of sophisticated suppliers in the world can build extensions onto an installed base without too many problems. The user has to make choices about the size of the system, but alterations in scale do not imply a qualitative change in the technology. The main issues suppliers and users need to resolve are therefore straightforward: there has to be an agreed definition of the size of the system, and arrangements for efficient transfer of technical information.

Other technologies can have extremely complicated internal architectures. The common manufacturing production system being introduced across six bottling plants by Albion Spirits (AS), discussed in the previous chapter, is a good example. Unlike an APCS in a distillery or an oil refinery, the boundaries of the system are not at all clear-cut. It must retain enough flexibility to be reconfigured as future company circumstances or technical advances in the field permit, and it must communicate with a number of other information systems. Where the decision to acquire the APCS in the distillery turned largely around technical function, a manufacturing control system introduced across a number of plants forces a user to concentrate on applications, since the relationship of the manufacturing system to other information systems has to be central to the acquisition. From the user viewpoint, an APCS is one-stop shopping, with a single supplier providing the equipment. The range of technical functions, applications, subsidiary information systems and communications protocols needed in a manufacturing system, however, are so great that few suppliers could provide all the equipment and expertise necessary. In this case, increasing the scale of the system does involve a qualitative change in the technology.

The nature of the user–supplier relationship is therefore partly conditioned by the internal architectures of the technologies involved. These can be simple even when the technology is complex. The key question is whether extending the system involves a quantitative or a qualitative change in technology. Where it involves a quantitative change, user–supplier relationships are simpler, revolving around technical function, and users will tend to have stable relationships with established suppliers. Where, as is increasingly the case, the internal architecture of a technology is complex and its applications are still only hazily defined, users are centrally concerned with applications and the number of potential suppliers is usually greater: hardware and software can be purchased from different suppliers, for example. As companies acquire new systems, they will tend to expand their supplier portfolio in the process. The management of expertise becomes inextricably tied up with the management of relationships with suppliers, simultaneously the most obvious and the most nakedly self-interested external source of expertise.

The nature of the marketplace

In broad terms, with the usual caveats about the difficulties of generalising about a market made up of so many sub-markets as the computer systems sector, it is the level of maturity in the market which most directly affects the balance of power between users and suppliers. On the whole, the more mature the market, the more the balance of power will favour users. The most important change favouring users in a maturing market is the greater choice of suppliers they have, a function of the expansion and specialisation characteristic of a maturing market. With increasing specialisation encouraging fragmentation into niche markets, the level of competition between suppliers increases: established companies with large product lines are attacked piecemeal by specialised suppliers. This kind of market backdrop is a precondition for the aggressive management of suppliers by users, since a ready alternative minimises disruption when suppliers are replaced and forces existing suppliers to offer advantageous terms to retain customers. The saving grace for suppliers is the high pace of innovation in the sector, which allows innovating companies to establish themselves, for a time, as the sole supplier of a certain product. As long as their lead lasts, they can dictate terms to users to a large extent.

The balance of expertise

When a transaction involves a notably complex technology, as those in the computer systems marketplace often do, the balance of expertise between user and supplier is a very important determinant of the balance of power between them. We have sketched out the two extremes in this and previous chapters: on the one hand, an immature market, with expertise focused on function and the balance of expertise favouring suppliers; on the other, a mature market, with expertise focused on applications and the balance of expertise favouring users. Between these two poles, however, there is an almost infinite series of gradations.

The level of expertise in users and suppliers is a critical variable in the relationship. Where transactions involve analysis of system requirements, organisational innovation, training, repairs and maintenance work, they are about the acquisition of managerial and technical expertise as much as about equipment acquisition. Many of the third parties playing an increasingly important structural role in computer systems markets and transactions – software houses and consultants, for example – sell expertise rather than specific boxes or systems: they are routinely pulled in by either suppliers or users to compensate for perceived imbalances in expertise during a trans-action. Thus in assessing the balance of expertise between users and suppliers, it is important not to restrict the analysis to them. Both also have a network of third-party relationships from which expertise is drawn.

It will be remembered that the definition of expertise we introduced in Chapter 2 stressed both specialist knowledge and its embodiment in work practices. The balance of expertise between supplier and user rests on two factors which refer back to the technical and operational components of what we understand as expertise. The first is degree of technical specialisation. The extent to which company personnel are able to command the specialised forms in which technical knowledge comes, its language, functional detail and engineering implications, is an important determinant of the extent to which it will be able to look after its interests in transactions concerning high technology acquisitions. But in addition to technical specialisation, there is also an operational factor: familiarity with applications. The marked difference in the balance of expertise between a supplier and an applications novice, as opposed to a veteran, was encapsulated in the way the sales representative who sold the APCS to AS compared these newcomers to the technology with his other account, one of the oil majors:

Albion Spirits had no experience of distributed control systems, and therefore some of the concepts were very difficult for them to take on board. . . . We are talking about distributed software and distributed hardware and distributed database managers, all of which provide features they couldn't have before. And I think it is true to say that they have had some difficulty in taking that aboard. . . . With Albion Spirits we now have somebody, in the form of Janet Smith, who understands several systems. But if we went to talk to some of the oil majors, the chances are high that the person sitting opposite you would have a good under-standing not only of your systems, but three of your competitors. . . . You have to look at the structure of an oil company. I mean, I don't honestly know how many process control engineers BP have, but it is in the hundreds. So we are comparing one or two engineers with hundreds, and these hundreds are in specific disciplines, extremely well qualified, and some with many, many years of experience. It is a different world to us.

It is obviously true that, the larger the company, the more suppliers are likely to give it special treatment. Nevertheless, it would be an over-simplification to say that size is the only determinant of the balance of expertise between user and supplier. It is common for the balance of expertise to be strongly in favour of a small supplier if the piece of equipment, or the type of expertise, is in strong demand. This is the case, for example, with suppliers of workstations. This is a market which has historically been dominated by smaller companies which beat corporate giants like IBM to the technology in the first place, and have since managed to retain market share in the face of competition from larger companies.

The rest of this chapter will examine how companies have attempted to manage user–supplier relationships as they buy or sell computer techno-logies, looking in particular at how they have attempted to manage expertise. It describes and analyses confrontational and collaborative approaches which were observed during field research. But our analysis differs in one important respect from previous examinations of the topic. We began this chapter with the observation that the user–supplier relationship is in reality two sub-relationships, user–supplier and supplier-user. It follows that the perspectives of both user and supplier need to be incorporated into the analysis for it to be complete. When training an analytical telescope on user–supplier relationships, it is necessary to look through both ends.

THE VIEW FROM THE SUPPLIER

A securely established long-term collaborative relationship with a customer is the holy grail of high-technology suppliers. It is the nearest a supplier can come to complete control of uncertainty, since it guarantees steady revenues: the pace of innovation in the sector forces users, whether original equipment manufacturers (OEMs) buying in disk drives or firms with significant investment in IT systems, to update their technical base periodically in order to stay competitive. Where the buyer is blue-chip, such as a large multinational, suppliers will go to extraordinary lengths to establish a collaborative relationship. A few years ago, one of the largest British multinationals sent out a letter to the major international suppliers of distributed process control systems (DPCS), around a dozen companies in all. It notified them that it had decided to appoint three authorised vendors of these systems to its plants worldwide, and invited them to apply for the honour. The application process consisted of the DPCS supplier turning over one of its plants to run a year-long trial of one of the systems under the multinational's supervision. If the outcome was satisfactory – and the suppliers were warned that the testing would cost around £1 million – they were then expected to allow the multinational full access to its books, undergo a complete financial audit, and submit its senior management to intensive interviewing by the multinational's executives. In other words, it was not just the technical characteristics of the supplier's systems which were being evaluated, but the financial and organisational integrity of the company. Despite the severity of these conditions, about half of the suppliers agreed to submit themselves to these organisational indignities. The manager who told us this story said it was like the check-up run on somebody marrying into the British royal family, without the discreetness.

The time, energy and effort spent on nurturing a long-term relationship with a user can be very high indeed, and lends itself well to the dominant metaphor used by senior management in suppliers to describe organisational relationships with users: human relationships.

> We were on on-site and that was the important thing. We had our successes but we also had our difficulties and problems with them, and I don't think one should play that down. It would be wrong and unnatural and untrue to play that down, because everyone knows there are these sorts of times. But we got through those with previous projects, we got things right, we stuck with them, and that's been a policy of SIE, it has to be. So we stuck with them through thick and thin, and we got good intelligence with them when that site came up.
>
> (Smith Instruments & Engineering sales representative)

As this quote implies, suppliers see the construction of a truly collaborative relationship with users as a long-term enterprise. To attain the state of grace where 'we got good intelligence from them when that site came up' is not something which can be developed overnight. It depends on the ability of individuals in the supplier to develop social relationships with user personnel, and such ties may take years to develop. The supplier personnel who are specifically detailed to create these relationships are mainly salespeople, although the word sales is unlikely to appear in their job-title: 'account manager' is a more typical job title for the salesperson in a company seeking strategic partnerships with customers, and, as these representatives will point out if you make the mistake of calling them salespeople, there is a difference:

> I don't have the title of salesman, though; I have the title of account

manager. That is a difference in emphasis that is very deliberate. In my early career we were known as 'sales' whatever, but today it is account manager. . . . I am an account manager, but, truthfully, the transaction is a sale.

It is not difficult to find sales representatives who have been managing the same account for decades, selling successive generations of technology to a company with which they become intimately familiar. As we have seen, these relationships between the salesforce of the supplier and cultivated individuals in the user are one of the most important feedback loops transmitting user experience of products to suppliers. But they also provide the intelligence suppliers require even in the most stable collaborative relationship. The ideal, as somebody who had been selling to Albion Spirits since the 1960s explained, is to be involved at the pre-tender stage, achieving such close interaction that 'perfect collaboration' – where differences in work practices between supplier and user melt away – becomes imaginable:

> That is one of the goals. If we can have them talking our language, to put it simply, to talk in the way that we do and to even engineer that way, now that would be useful.

However, certain preconditions need to be met before suppliers will consider committing the human and material resources which the construction of long-term collaborative relationships implies. The first is that systems and expertise sold have to be high value, to compensate for the time and effort involved. They are not found in the low-value, high-volume end of markets. The type of company most interested in forming collaborative relationships is typically a large or medium-sized international company, or a niche supplier. In niche markets the number of suppliers is by definition not large, and unless suppliers are sole owners of a system or expertise in high demand, they will seek to form collaborative relationships with users because of the much higher overheads involved in relying on new business rather than installed base. They are also highly dependent on user intelligence to be able to continue to innovate in their product area.

The second precondition is that the level of competition between suppliers should not be cut-throat. Suppliers need to feel reasonably sure that a collaborative relationship with a user will be stable enough over time for it to be worth their while. This will not often be the case in markets driven solely by price, where the tendency of suppliers to undercut one another is exacerbated by their being played off against each other by aggressive customers. It also follows that collaborative relationships depend to an extent on the general economic environment. In a recession, suppliers compete against each other more desperately than during periods of growth, and will undercut each other more readily. Any economic downturn puts collaborative user–supplier relationships under strain.

Finally, only certain kinds of business organisation are capable of constructing long-term collaborative relationships with customers. They need 'account managers' or other personnel who have dealt with customers long enough and closely enough to supply reliable detail about the firm's organisational structure, plans, timetables, work practices and personnel changes. This imposes constraints on the supplier. There needs to be a degree of stability in the personnel dealing directly with customers, which can be difficult to achieve in high-technology sectors when experts move with ease between companies in a labour market where their skills are in high demand: it is easier to keep sales staff stable than it is to hang on to R&D engineers. Ideally, in the key interstitial roles like sales, the same people should deal with the customer for many years. This implies well-defined job boundaries in the supplier, since it would be disorienting for the buyers' representatives to be dealing with continually changing members of a supplier team. It follows that the collaboratively inclined supplier will operate with a clear separation of departmental roles. This is an organisational feature more commonly associated with the mechanistic than with the organically structured firm. An important implication is that, if we want to understand the internal structure of a company, we should recognise that this is in part determined by the senior management's perceptions of the appropriate style of supply chain relationships, given their interpretation of the market. There is not, in other words, a simple best fit between an external, objective economic context and the structure of the firm. The relationship is instead mediated by the socially constructed notions of the senior figures in the firm hierarchy, and their willingness and ability to direct change.

Although social networks between supplier and user generally result from a collaborative relationship, it is senior management, and not salespeople or technical experts, who decide to enter into formal collaboration or strategic partnership with a supplier. The supplier will seek to institutionalise the relationship as far as possible, believing that the existence of organisational mechanisms in which both suppliers and users are represented is a guarantee of permanence. But the existence of these forums can sometimes blind one to the inherent power relationship. What looks like collaboration can often be the result of essentially confrontational approaches towards suppliers by users. One example is represented by the interventionism that suppliers submit to from powerful users as part of the active supply-chain management prescribed by JIT and TQM, where suppliers compete for formal nomination as approved or authorised vendors and then work extremely closely with customers at all organisational levels. While this has advantages in some contexts, from the supplier viewpoint it has disadvantages too. It reduces managerial autonomy, and may result in over-dependence on a single dominant user, which can be disastrous if the user decides to alter or rationalise its supply chain, or drive down costs, both common strategies in a recession.

However, such clear-cut institutionalised collaboration remains the exception. From the supplier's point of view, most collaborative agreements with customers seem institutionally fragile, and constantly liable to slide back towards the confrontational end of the axis. However diligently senior management cultivate their opposite numbers and encourage contact between their own and customer personnel through bodies like user groups, they run up against the problem that – with some exceptions – senior managers in users are not stupid. They are alive to the self-interested nature of invitations to golfing weekends and the like from suppliers, to which they respond with a mixture of cynicism and opportunism. And there is the further problem of the fundamental unpredictability of the business world: suppliers may successfully set up institutional forums with users only to have their work made irrelevant by an external event. We saw in the case of AS how an external event, like a takeover, can transform a relationship from long-established, inertial collaboration to intense competition almost overnight.

In addition, suppliers will often find themselves having to deal not just with customers, but also with third parties – consultants or other technical specialists – brought in precisely to avoid over-dependence on supplier expertise. While supplier managers and sales representatives, unsurprisingly, tend to have a low opinion of consultants,

> they sit on the fence a great deal, tend to use a huge amount of capital in doing so, and then walk away, hand the plan over and say here are fifteen solutions, take your pick, if you want us to do it please can we have more money.
>
> (TE sales manager)

they have no option but to grin and work with them. One practice which has become common when large systems acquisitions are made is for users to set up business teams with the participation of consultants to define specifications, select a supplier and manage implementation. As a result, suppliers find themselves unable to set up a straightforward one-to-one collaborative relationship. Instead they have to function in a mediated relationship, which can be collaborative or confrontational, and generally has elements of both. In any mediated relationship, it is more difficult for the supplier to create the dependence on products and expertise from which its revenues are generated.

Ironically the most technically complicated form of collaboration tends to be the least problematic for suppliers. When a supplier makes a computer system sale, successful implementation often depends on the exchange of a mass of technical information between supplier and user. This is carried out by technical specialists from supplier and user attached to project management teams, working together closely. It can create problems when there is an imbalance of expertise between the parties, as is often the case with a user buying a particular technology for the first time. This was the case with the distributed process control system acquired by Albion Spirits, and it caused some problems for the Smith Instruments & Engineering project manager:

> The [implementation] schedule, as well as defining our commitments and when we will deliver, also has to define the information we need and when we need that information. That's one of the critical things, I think, between us and the client, is specifying the information they have to give us to allow us to build the system. They have to give us that information. ... They've not been able to give us that on the original timescale. ... Although Albion are fairly large, they are primarily a process manufacturing company, and it doesn't have all the engineering support it needs at a time like this. ... In some of the smaller companies there may even be lack of expertise at the process control side ... we try and get together with them. We in fact did this with Albion, showed them standard engineering documents of the type we could use that would provide the information we needed.

As this episode suggests, technical collaboration is relatively simple, because there are defined technical solutions to problems. It is not usually very difficult for suppliers to educate users in them, if necessary. It is simply a case of facilitating information flows, which is usually easily accomplished by dialogue between technical experts over common ground. Managers in suppliers must often wish that all the organisational issues related to collaboration were as easily resolvable.

THE COLLABORATIVE SALES STRATEGY –
A SUPPLIER CASE STUDY

During the past decade TE has sought, through its sales organisation, to promote new forms of collaborative user–supplier relationships. The difference between the old and the new approach can be summed up as the contrast between selling boxes (hardware and software) and selling 'added value', or the intangibles of knowledge and expertise. Both may involve long-term relationships between supplier and customer, but the latter is inherently dependent on the cultivation of close links with users. Sales work has become more segmented, and a distinct division of labour has evolved between social 'front' and technical 'back stage' roles.

TE's product range is traditionally divided into two broad categories: instrumentation and commercial systems. In fact the diffusion of micro-electronics and the increasing use of UNIX-based solutions in commercial as well as technical systems has blurred the distinction, but at the time of our research the sales organisation remained structured on these lines. For our purposes it provides a useful contrast between old and new styles of selling, as indicated in Figure 2.

Instrumentation sales represent the traditional approach to selling technical equipment. In this sector, TE has always been and continues to be a market leader; hence it is self-assured and relaxed in its approach despite

| | Product range | |
	Instrumentation and analytic tools	Business and commercial systems/information integration
Type of sale	Engineer to engineer end-user; sold on technical performance and intrinsic value to the user who sells up the hierarchy to senior management	Consultative approach to senior management; sold on value to the business, by provision of financial justification not value to end-user; top-down sale
Role of technical specialists in user	Equals, allies and supporters doing sales work for the supplier; educator to the supplier on product development, because of technical acumen.	Potential foe and betrayer; threat to future relationship; defensive because of own career agenda
Division of expertise in seller	Integral technical and social roles	Division of social and technical roles: sales representatives are the front team with commercial knowhow; technical specialists occupy the back room and provide the technical solutions;

Figure 2 Telewave Electronics sales organisation

increasing challenges from smaller competitors. Long-standing customers, who provide the major part of revenues, are assumed to be basically friendly and unlikely to throw the sales representatives off the account. The market is relatively speaking a known quantity: there are very few completely new customers and sales staff work with the same user engineers for many years. Relationships thus follow an inertial form of collaboration. The sales role is predominantly a technical one, and is in social terms altogether simpler than that involved in selling commercial systems. The transaction is between technical equals who are commonly known to each other or who can act as though they are members of a common community. In line with product values ranging from hundreds of pounds to over a million, the contract may be sealed at a number of levels, from technician to managing director. The concentration of sales effort is at the technical level, however. Division managers or directors are unlikely to be involved in the specifics of the supply contract, whatever its cost: 'nobody pretends to know much about measurements and would much prefer not to be involved' (TE sales engineer). TE representatives were of course keen to emphasise that this did not mean complacent inaction on their part: 'you cannot afford to take the short-term view. Whatever you promote to the customer has to be in his long-term best interests' (sales engineer). Customers are knowledgeable about the products because they operate in similar business sectors and talk the same language. Feedback on product performance and customer input into product development is mainly informal, because of continuing contact with the same engineers. When the sales representative feels the need to involve development engineers, in the interest of promoting future generations of sales, he will put pressure on the appropriate TE factory to set up a site visit for the customer engineers.

Much of the instrumentation business continues to be dependent on selling boxes rather than systems, although custom-built systems play an increasing part in the generation of sales. In Britain some of TE's largest, most complex systems have been built for Defence Electronics and there was a long-standing friendly relationship between engineers in the two companies. Such sales transactions could span a five year period, as the supplier's test and measurement packages are developed alongside the user's new production schedules. The in-house expertise necessary to develop such systems was proving increasingly valuable as a tactic to stave off competition from smaller suppliers. Technical expertise in the sales representative therefore was regarded as vital to continuing success. The supplier's representatives had to be able to talk to other engineers who were similar in background and experience: 'what our guys have to do is educate our customers on what the latest box can do . . . ongoing updating our customers' technological skills' (technical sales manager). Their expertise was acquired in part by in-house training, but regular contact with customer engineers and the recruitment of engineers with experience in the specific markets into which TE sells were at least as important. Many instrumentation sales representatives were ex-customer engineers who had been sold to by an earlier generation of TE representatives: 'I'd say that the majority of people in instrumentation have practised as engineers, working for the sort of people who are our customers' (TE sales engineer). Recruitment of engineers into sales was not straightforward, however, regardless of the attractions of a high salary. Most engineers regarded sales as 'a slightly doubtful occupation' (TE sales engineer) and had to be enticed into it not just by money but by recruitment techniques which stressed the technical content of the work.

The technical approach to selling, as practised in TE, is a clear example of inertial collaboration. The profit motive is institutionalised through the respective sales and purchasing functions in the producer and the user, but the engineering functions on both sides may get together behind the scenes to ensure that their work, and their relationship with technical peers, is not disrupted. This way of operating may result in a quotient of 'guilty knowledge' shared between the engineers on both sides and serving to bind them together even more firmly (Hughes, 1971). A TE marketing manager gave us an example of this when talking about the tendering process:

> We get the case where a customer will be obliged to provide a tender to multiple people ... but he may well want to buy from TE. ... We very often get tenders ... asking us to modify ... the terms of it ... so that you can guarantee to get the business. ... We have worked very closely with customers attempting to write a spec for a piece of equipment ... I know it's immoral or illegal ... I don't think it is. ... Some of the reasons are that large companies will have separate people doing technical evaluations on products from those doing pricing. ... The buyers are charged with going in to find the lowest priced product. It may be the technical department knows exactly what they want. ... So they have to find a way to ensure that the buyers buy what they want ... so they are obliged to find some way to modify the specification ... and they find it easier to work with us. It is a matter of final distinction between who is ultimately going to use it. ... (and) who is going to write the cheque.

Unlike the selling of instrumentation and measurement systems, the selling of business systems is a good example of the attempt by suppliers to build new forms of strategic collaboration with customers. This sale is targeted at director level and is consequently not between status or technical equals. The cost of the system is typically (though not necessarily) far greater and the business implications on both sides correspondingly more significant. The metaphor which springs to mind for the developing sales expertise in the computer systems sphere is that of AIDS and the new sexual morality. The old-school sales approach could be characterised as one night stands: 'quick kill and run' or 'sell it thin and get it in', as TE sales managers described the sales philosophy of some competitors. Money was like sex in the pre-AIDS era: the objective was to get as much as possible in the shortest possible time. The new sales vocabulary talks of partnership, trust, monogamy, a warm, caring dependence, heart to heart support and 'healing of the raw nerves of the business' (TE support engineer). New style selling certainly does not involve open wrangling over the sordid details of price, which appears to have become taboo in certain styles of selling. Indeed too great a fixation on price by the customer was regarded as a kind of moral failing, as was a confrontational approach to managing suppliers:

> There is one large electronics company which is well known for having purchasing people whose job it is to screw the suppliers down to the absolute bare bones. It is a very foolish thing to do. Generally the supplier will be in a position not long afterwards to get some leverage back and recoup the money.

> (Sales manager)

Elaborating the social dimension in commercial sales work

If a supplier is to develop a form of strategic collaboration with customers, that supplier has to change the customer's perception of what is being bought and sold. In particular, the buyer has to be persuaded that, in exchange for privileged access, the supplier has something worth trading, beyond mere equipment. In TE's case, instead of boxes, or hardware and software in system form, the objective is to sell 'added value' to the customer in the form of solutions to problems and the promise of improved business performance. Added value is essentially intangible. TE representatives, if asked what they were selling, replied 'I sell added value'. And what is added value? 'The added value of any system is knowledge.' The supplier has to put substance on the bones of such a concept to convince the customer that there is something here worth paying for:

> We're not selling computers, we're selling money ... we are really saying we can provide solutions that will put X amount on your bottom line. ... The fact that we use this technology to do it is to some extent irrelevant to a finance director, as long as he believes what you're saying is true ... we are actually selling money.

> (TE sales representative)

Selling computer systems in this way involves telling the customer what is best for its business and setting the terms for making such assessments. It is first and foremost not a technical sale, but is about establishing the reputation and social worth of the would-be supplier, who aims to cultivate the self-presentation of morally perfect provider of solutions:

> it is establishing TE as a reputable computer supplier to that organisation that is my primary objective. . . . So I very rarely get involved in discussions about what computers can and cannot do. . . . I get involved in business discussion as to what people want to do with computers. . . . And that's all to do with the application rather than the bits and bytes and megaflips and megaflops. . . . That is the way the business has changed in the past few years.
>
> (Account manager)

> TE are trying to generate a culture of honesty, commitment and all those good nice words. But they actually mean something in TE. . . . We don't want to sell something knowingly that is not going to fulfil the objectives that we have jointly settled . . . or that we have claimed.
>
> (Account manager)

There is nothing new in the principle of selling systems to improve business performance. What is new is the way the principle is applied:

> Instead of saying here is a computer that costs X . . . and leaving it to the customer to decide whether the combination of hardware and software constitutes a computer system . . . the [TE view] is that we should understand that business and we should be able to say to the customer, if you install our system it will have this effect on your margins.
>
> (Account manager)

One account manager described this process as 'the installation of our expertise which happens to include our computer system'. Centres of business expertise were being created in TE to provide the sort of commercial knowledge which sales people increasingly relied on to demonstrate their competence. The more they were able to provide examples drawn from successful applications in other companies in the same industry, the more the customer was impressed:

> We are building up centres of expertise within TE, and these centres are collating all their experience in the chemical industry, in the food industry, in the pharmaceutical business, in the finance business, in the defence business, in the transportation business . . . and therefore we would look to use those guys. . . . The knowledge base we are building up on X is something other computer companies will never have and

therefore it increasingly becomes the means by which the customer stays with us. As you are probabaly aware, there is a move towards systems which are industry standard and therefore the differentiation afforded to the manufacturers by their technology has been taken away. Now that is being replaced by knowledge and people.

(Account manager)

For the supplier the development of such industry expertise offers a way of getting entrenched in the user's business:

If you are looking at a company like us to provide competitive edge, you have got to get to the heart of the business and once you get to the heart of the business you are very very difficult to dislodge.

(Account manager)

Strategic collaboration and the division of labour in the sales team

Unlike instrumentation sales engineers, commercial systems representatives did not necessarily come from an engineering background. The desirable skills were seen not in technical terms but in social terms. What the sales representatives needed was the ability to talk their way into senior levels of a company and explain in convincing terms the value of TE systems to profitability:

A lot of it is down to personal relationships, a lot of my business is down to the trust that you build up with people.

(Account manager)

Not surprisingly, specialist roles were used to handle different categories of customer. There was a prominent division between those representatives working with existing customers ('installed base') and those targeting new business. The latter could spend up to three years courting a potential customer, selected for the scale of its investment in new technology but currently committed to another supplier. Targeted companies were operating in an identified business sector, such as food, drink and tobacco, which TE aimed to sell into. Over a number of years the objective was to research the business and convince the target companies of the potential contribution to be made by strategic collaboration with TE. One of our informants had already spent two years courting the attentions of senior management in Albion Spirits, with only limited success. The two sales roles, new accounts and installed base, had acquired something of a masculine–feminine distinction. Sales representatives working on new business, all of them male, were seen as needing tenacity, determination, boundless self-confidence and self-motivation, the ability to work in a very individualistic way to 'kick down doors' and the ease of mind to cope with no visible results for a year or more whilst staying on talking to the target. Conversely they also had to know when to cut their losses and walk away. The qualities required in those looking after existing accounts were described in classically feminine terms: attention to detail, ability to communicate, give guidance, work well in a team and not antagonise people. The one woman sales representative in the team was predictably working with existing accounts.

The sales front team, as opposed to the technical back-room support they could call on, had to be applied ethnographers in their own right. Considerable emphasis was placed on accurate and detailed local knowledge – knowing what the customer was planning, what the competition was doing, the ins and outs of inter-company politics, sales tactics and the relative technical strengths and weaknesses of competing products. This kind of expertise was regarded as central to success in the negotiation of a contract. Knowledge of the customer means being able to distinguish between a real sales opportunity and a hopeless situation. Effective activity was described as getting in to talk to the person who has the power to write the cheque: ' "it's only for rubber stamping" are famous last words . . . call wide and high' (sales manager). The representative has to know the timescales the client is working to, the budget they have and the role of any third parties working for them. Knowledge of the competition is particularly relevant to the delicate discount pricing decisions which may be necessary to win a valuable contract. The sales process, in other words, is studied in immense detail. In addition back-room technical support is brought in to specify, with the customer, the engineering detail of the proposed system. Such technical experts were also expected to be able to talk convincingly to all levels in the company, from board level to engineer to end user, and to be able to identify some of the potential organisational barriers to a successful deal as well as the technical requirements of the system: a role somewhat akin to marriage guidance!

The self-conceptions of job occupants

Sales representatives were actively engaged in upgrading their conception of themselves and their work. This was an enterprise in which they were helped by a widespread perception among senior and corporate management that TE had relied too much in the past on a reputation for engineering excellence and needed to emphasise marketing and sales if it was to fight off new competitors. The representatives were thus placed in a simultaneously powerful, and difficult, role. They were in a position to do considerable damage to both the customer's and the supplier's business. In order to bring about strategic collaboration, the supplier minimally has to revise the customer's conceptions of the sales role, from 'a slightly doubtful occupation' to a profession. The objective of going 'to the heart of the business' is an aspiration which requires the licence and mandate of the professions, with their metaphorical clean hands and a demonstrable possession of valued technical knowledge. The movement to professionalise was a form of collective mobility for sales staff, as they attempted to eradicate the association of selling with 'dirty tricks' and deception. This is no easy task since it is an image which is deeply rooted in Western popular culture. The second-hand car salesman is a mythical figure in more ways than one. An indicator of professional aspirations was the use of formal titles which emphasised technical knowledge and business acumen; thus representatives were 'sales engineers' or 'account managers'. The struggle for the respect due to a profession was reflected in one representative's comment that she aimed to 'make sure the customers understand the value of what we are actually doing for them'. She wanted to see more recognition from customers of the benefits derived from the input of TE expertise. In exchange for a degree of autonomy, dignity and self-worth granted by senior management, sales representatives in turn protected the senior ranks from their mistakes: 'the buck stops here' (account manager). The representatives were given control over who had access to their clients and on what terms; engineers from factory or laboratory, for example, had to approach customers via the representative, not directly. A sense of dignity was not expected to be its own reward, however: proper commitment to the role was recompensed by a high salary, the greater part of which was guaranteed.

Handling the problems of mistakes and failures

Mistakes in computer system sales have fateful consequences for the customer because of the massive capital entailed. The sales role therefore has special problems of apprenticeship and access to relevant situations where the job can be learnt. In many ways sales is the opposite of R&D. It is the natural home of those wise in the ways of the world, who can be trusted to be let loose on senior managers in customer firms. Young graduates are regarded as a hazard and are kept as errand runners for a number of years or expected to serve an apprenticeship in a support role elsewhere in the company. Youthfulness is altogether an undesirable quality in the pseudo-consultative style, which requires the representative to analyse business problems and convince senior managers that they know the weaknesses in a firm's operation better than the managers do themselves, as well as being able to offer a solution: 'a 23 year old can't pull that off' (sales manager).

When mistakes do occur, the team develops its own rationales and defences in order to deal with them and to be able to continue working. Routines and procedures were constructed as a means of 'doing a proper job' and protecting sales representatives from fears of failure. The following of set procedures allowed them to claim that the deal was properly handled, whatever the outcome. These depended heavily on the consultative style of selling and the use of a device described as the profit improvement proposal, 'the mechanism by which added value is conveyed to the customer ... what you sell to a customer is improved profit, nothing else' (TE account manager). A distinction was made between successful and professionally correct handling of a sale. If the work was 'done properly', it allowed responsibility for relative failure to be placed on the user's business contingencies, despite the user's natural desire to blame the supplier. Notably, an explicit aspect of the appraisal system in use for sales representatives was evidence of 'a clean organisation'.

So what constituted proper handling? The first important step was getting in at the right level – senior management – and bypassing the in-house technical or data processing function. To get stuck at data processing level was seen as a threat to successful handling of a sale:

> You are always under threat within that account that somebody at a more senior level will then think that the technology in that organisation is not assisting the business and maybe they should get another supplier. . . . Somebody might suddenly come in on the sly . . . and you are always in the weak position.
>
> (Sales representative)

Equally important was the setting of user expectations. Ideally this was achieved by pre-sales consultancy by the supplier which the user paid for. Everyone was well aware that a company spending perhaps tens of thousands of pounds on such consultancy was already halfway committed to the TE system. Convincing a customer that such pre-sales work was worth paying for was not of course straightforward:

> I would see that an essential part of the process would be to convince the customer that the production of the profit improvement proposal will give him the means by which he can measure the success of his installation and therefore he should pay for it. . . . This goes against the grain for a lot of businessmen, actually paying us to do a proposal to say whether or not we should sell to them.
>
> (TE account manager)

The setting of expectations about system performance was thus central to avoiding accusations of failure and mistakes. Ideally an internal IT liaison person was an ally, rather than an obstacle, in this process, helping to set expectations and forestalling difficult meetings later on.

If all else failed, there were routines for cooling out the user. This was regarded as the toughest part of the job and the dirtiest work a representative had to do. The sales team tried to lay claim to the right to define when a mistake or failure had occurred. In structural terms, the division of labour between the sales representatives, who uphold the moral front, and the technical back-room team who are the repository of 'the knowledge' was highly valuable in this process. The technical experts could be called on for their expertise without threatening the reputation of the sales front person. The TE expert was sent in to conduct a combined technical and organisational analysis. He or she reported to a project team. The user frequently contested their authority. Hence it is difficult to do research on alleged failures because of the feeling the representatives have that outsiders cannot fully appreciate the context of risks and contingencies involved. Such events may not even be discussed openly within the sales team and may become a source of hidden anxieties, denied to outsiders.

Failure was regarded as more likely to occur when the customer firm had a complex structure, with pockets of IT expertise in different systems and applications, located unpredictably around the organisation, or where the number of interested parties was more than two. The location of the main stumbling block, as far as TE representatives were concerned, was a traditional data processing function in the user's organisation. TE representatives favoured those companies who were seeking to distribute IT expertise throughout the business rather than centralising it in a functional department. Ideally, they wanted to deal with information systems managers who viewed the business as driving IT strategy rather than the other way round. Those companies where computing was 'in an ivory tower' with members who 'still want to write Cobol programmes', who view the user as 'the bane of their life' and who are enthused primarily by the latest technical tricks (TE technical support), were viewed as sites where aggressive negotiations were likely. As far as TE representatives were concerned, such people's private career agendas could result in the blocking of a sale, because of their predisposition to another vendor. A centralised data processing function also posed structural problems since the supplier could get pigeonholed at this level, instead of being able to achieve the aim of roaming freely across the organisational hierarchy, allowing them to 'become more built in with the bricks' (sales representative) and more difficult to dislodge. In such cases, it was harder for the supplier to control the setting of user expectations:

> [when] the selling process [is] from the internal technical people to the users; they oversell the system often to get it justified and then we are struggling to deliver everything to that expectation.
>
> (Sales representative)

This was especially hard to handle when it was the expectations of senior managers that were not being met: the in-house technical people would often fail to handle them as smoothly as the TE representatives would have liked. They preferred a direct channel to senior managers through, for example, representatives on a project management team. Sales representatives could also find themselves mediating the competing allocations of blame between a software designer, a hardware supplier and an in-house technical department. Either way, the response was the same: call on the TE back-room support engineers to provide evidence of the root of the failure, by appointing a 'problem manager'. The senior managers in the user would then be faced with the TE technical representative explaining that the company (not the system) had a 'performance difficulty'. Lack of technical expertise in the user, as we have seen, was treated as relatively easy to compensate for. A lack of organisational and management expertise, on the other hand, made for a difficult sale. When things go wrong, however, the advantage of the social construction of the sales process is that it is almost infinitely capable of shifting the blame onto somebody else. Conversely, regardless of the skills of the negotiators on either side, there is always likely to be a degree of ambivalence in the relationship, and caution about what each party stands to gain or lose. Hence there is never 'perfect collaboration'.

For TE, being more responsive to user needs and demands was not simply a matter of product innovation, but also meant reconstructing the sales process, away from inertial forms of collaboration, as had been the norm in instrumentation, and away from the technical approach to business systems sales in the commercial sphere. The driving force behind the change in the sales process appears to have been change in both technology and market context. In a nutshell, the movement from centralised data processing functions and mainframe computing to distributed computing with industry standard operating systems means that the technology no longer differentiates the suppliers. Consequently, in order to survive, suppliers have had to find something else to give them a competitive base. Increasingly, for TE, this meant developing sales as a form of user consultancy, seeking to solve the problems of the customer's business operations by the application of IT. This strategy was not without its problems. For one thing, TE managers had to recruit people into sales with the ability to handle both technical knowledge of products and business knowledge of the sector they were selling into and the social knowhow to talk convincingly to senior managers. The developing division of labour was focusing on the sales generalist, dealing with the customer, backed up by behind-the-scenes technical experts in support teams and specialist business experts, located in 'centres of expertise'. For the customer, the promise of ready-made IT solutions to business problems was no doubt both tempting and viewed with a degree of scepticism. TE representatives had a reputation, with our informants, for honesty and integrity, but all the same there was some doubt that they had the business acumen to deliver on promises. They were still regarded as lacking in their marketing abilities. For the supplier, therefore, representatives had to walk a tightrope between over-promising and setting customer expectations at a manageable level. Providing a technical fix was the least of their problems. Handling the social situation was far more difficult, particularly in customers lacking managerial and organisational competence. A supplier dedicated to this form of strategic collaboration with users is likely to encounter most problems dealing with companies structured on 'mechanistic' or segmented lines, with a centralised data processing department and a specialist buying function rewarded for price control. In other words a collaborative sales strategy and a segmented structure in the buyer is a recipe for problems and failures.

THE VIEW FROM THE USER

If strategic collaboration is an ideal for many high-technology suppliers, for many customers it is a more ambiguous, double-edged option. In deciding whether to follow confrontational or collaborative strategies towards suppliers, certain variables play a very obvious role. Size is the most obvious: the larger the company, the more it is able to make suppliers dance to its tune, as we saw in the case of the oil major and suppliers of distributed process control systems. Large buyers can be as confrontational as they like in managing their supplier relationships, knowing that the potential market they represent will ensure they are courted by suppliers irrespective of how they are treated. They may of course choose to pursue collaborative relationships, for strategic reasons. Buyers who are not the IBMs and ICIs of this world face the problem of needing to tap into the pool of expertise contained in a supplier without being able to set the terms of the relationship unilaterally. Users know enough about the hard realities of business to cut through the rhetoric of collaboration and co-operation which accompanies some approaches from suppliers, and are aware of the danger of allowing themselves to become revenue milk-cows to suppliers. Nevertheless, depending on market context, the nature of the technology and the history of relationships with particular suppliers, users do enter into collaborative arrangements of various kinds, each one of which is distinguished by a different balance of power. Some supplier relationships are entered into freely; others are forced.

In certain contexts users have no option but to collaborate: when there is only one source of supply for a particular technology. When a supplier establishes a significant technical lead over the competition, users have to make the best arrangements they can, a situation characteristic of immature markets. Forced collaboration, with a user strategically bound to a monopoly supplier, is by no means unusual in the computer systems marketplace, with its high level of innovation. It is inherently uncomfortable for senior managers in the customer, intensely aware of over-dependence and the difficulties of achieving a satisfactory level of service from a supplier which knows its users have nowhere else to go. Albion Spirits, for example, had identified an information engineering system produced by a company called Delphi as central to its plans for changing the IT base of the company in the long term, and had incorporated it into their strategic plan for IT development. A senior manager in Information Services at Albion described the problems the monopoly supplier caused him in these gloomy terms, an attitude in contrast with the bullish confrontational approach he pursued with other suppliers:

> Delphi I find a very difficult relationship, because I can't fit a Delphi system with Acme [the installed information system], because we have a statement of direction with regard to how we are going to use Delphi [systems]. So it worried me, because as a result I see we do not get the performance that as a customer spending a million dollars plus worldwide with their organisation, we should have much more value added from them, which we don't get. They see us as, oh yes, we'll send them another three copies of their UNIX database, or whatever. And I don't know how we get round that. We are strategically bound to Delphi. They know it, I know it, and that process is being managed at the Albion–Delphi managing director level, on the basis that, hey, I like you, but my troops think you're dreadful. This may potentially lead us to reconsider our position. What are you going to do about it?

Unfortunately for Albion, the answer is probably not very much. Unless alternative sources of supply develop, there is no incentive for suppliers like Delphi to allow its users much say in setting the terms for collaboration. Confrontational strategies with suppliers are only possible in a market context which provides alternative sources of supply. While the pace of innovation in the sector does often resolve this kind of problem in time, users have the problem of being forced into disadvantageous supplier relationships at precisely the time when the technology offers the greatest competitive edge.

However, relationships where the balance of power is so lopsidedly on the side of either supplier or user are less numerous than those where the balance is more even. It is very often the case that users are dealt a certain hand by the marketplace, but can significantly improve – or worsen – the balance of power with a supplier by the purchasing and implementation strategies they follow, all of which ultimately revolve around the management of expertise. Customer firms pursuing a JIT/TQM philosophy, such as AS and TE, generally have an active policy of vendor management. They will seek to move away from *laissez-faire*, inertial supply contracts, with an inherited and sometimes unwieldy collection of suppliers, towards what are generally portrayed as 'strategic partnerships', with a deliberately selected, smaller group of suppliers. The intention of the buyer is to improve the quality of its bought-in technology, including making use of the vendor's expertise, implicitly or explicitly, as part of the contract. In the case of disk drives, for example, Midas was desperate to gain such contracts with buyers, because of the perception that such partnerships would increasingly determine the future of the disk-drive business. Buyers try to use such 'partnerships' to impose higher standards in relation to quality and price on suppliers, in exchange for a relatively stable source of revenues. At the other end of the supply chain, firms like AS, buying-in new IT systems on an extensive scale, also want guarantees of quality, cost control and exchange of expertise. By definition such partnerships are partly collaborative and partly adversarial: each side has some shared interest in completing the contract and some competing interest relating not just to the direct costs of a transaction but also to the subjective utilities in the exchange. Indeed, 'strategic partnerships', as conceived by the senior management of AS, implied keeping vendors on their toes and playing them off against each other, in order to ensure that they delivered on their promises. As far as AS was concerned, no supplier should hold such a major part of a system contract that they are able to set the terms. Size is of course all important. Suppliers are less keen to gather potentially arduous partnerships where the resulting revenues are small. Such users are below the level of notice of many big suppliers, who typically deal with small businesses through a network of indirect agents. The exception is where a supplier believes that a user offers a new technical challenge, which would result in innovations for the supplier and the opening of doors to valuable new business.

A very common strategy by users who consider themselves lacking in relevant systems expertise is to involve third parties to mediate supplier relationships. In these organisational *ménages à trois*, the third party – usually a consultant – plays a crucial role. They are mediators not just in the sense of acting as arbitrators of conflicts and confrontation between user and supplier, but also in the sense of providing an institutional medium within which users and suppliers can communicate, initially in a purchasing team and perhaps subsequently in a project management team overseeing implementation. For users, involving third parties in their supplier relationships has a hidden advantage – they are external people to blame if things go wrong. Bought-in expertise is not merely technical, but has important political and social functions. Users delegate to external agents not merely because of lack of expertise in how to assess the merits of suppliers of a technology new to them, or for advice about new technological applications in their business, but in part because of defensiveness over the possibility of error and having to face the anxiety of failure. Indeed perhaps the most common reason to involve a consultant is more to do with internal organisational politics. With the terms of reference set in such a way that a close fit between the consultant's verdict and a hidden agenda can be guaranteed, the 'impartial' recommendation becomes a convenient way of outflanking internal opposition. Third parties, and by extension the suppliers involved with the user on the recommendation or prompting of third parties, may become the fall guys rather than user management, avoiding divisive internal recriminations.

Of course, mediated supplier relationships bring a different set of problems to the user. Consultants are often viewed sceptically, with their lack of commitment to the user in the final analysis always borne in mind: they are regular butts of jokes by managers in users and suppliers – 'a consultant is somebody who borrows your watch to tell you the time, and then charges you for doing it'. Consultants are seen as being there to gain more consultancy business as much as anything: 'what he is doing is marketing a relationship which brings him more consultancy revenues' (TE sales representative). At the same time they are valued by buyers for being apparently more disinterested than suppliers; any attempt by suppliers to outflank them and deal directly with senior management arouses deep suspicions and hostility. TE sales managers, for example, were concerned to stay on the right side of consultants, who were regarded as gatekeepers of potential business: 'if you go behind their back . . . you end up offending them and they will not want to do busines with you' (TE sales manager).

CONCLUSION

If our informants are to be relied upon, the days of inertial forms of collaboration are numbered, but so are the days of the straightforwardly 'technical' approach to buying and selling, where the evaluation is solely on price and technical performance comparisons. We have to speculate of course on the extent to which such claims were rhetoric and aspiration, rather than reality. What we can assert with confidence is that there is a new awareness of the need to reassess the portfolio of supply chain relationships and their contribution to the profitability of the business. In practice, there is, in many firms, a gap between that awareness and the managerial ability to identify and enact appropriate changes.

Generalisations about users are difficult, since firms using computing technologies, either as part of their products or in controlling their work processes, cover just about every industrial sector and market context. In our own segment of a supply chain, we had Midas at one end, supplying disk drives predominantly to workstation manufacturers and using bought-in computing technology both in its products and processes. As a user, it was aware of the need to manage suppliers actively, but continuing internal crises and the inability of management to intervene in a cycle of falling revenues and rising debt meant that 'vendor management' was in practice *ad hoc* and a matter of fire-fighting from day to day. The demise of Midas was a source of great anxiety for many specialist suppliers, who relied on Midas orders for a significant part of their revenues. There was ample evidence that Midas was kept afloat for a number of years by the 'goodwill' of its suppliers. In such cases, friendships between buyer and supplier engineers, new technical challenges for suppliers and active vendor managers make the difference between riding out a difficult period and going out of business. In Midas's case, however, the failure of management to implement a workable strategy for the new environment eventually led to its demise. As a supplier, it failed to solve internal technical problems in design and manufacturing, and despite attempting to use the expertise of customers in product engineering it was unable to generate sufficient revenues to stay afloat. TE's workstation operation had used Midas to supply disk drives and was far more successful in its pursuit of active vendor management, claiming to have cut costs of components while improving quality. Its aim was not to inspect any goods on arrival, and not to have a high level of inventory of any parts, which meant a highly interventionist approach to selected suppliers to ensure the quality of their production engineering and the ability to set agreed production timetables. Such was the market power of TE and the perceived value of its engineering expertise that suppliers were keen to gain the status of 'authorised vendor'. As a supplier, TE was itself competing with computer systems suppliers for high-value 'strategic partnerships' with large IT users such as AS. Here TE in turn was having to develop new forms of expertise in business consultancy and marketing. For AS, prior to takeover, inertial collaboration with a computer systems supplier was so well established, and systems were sufficiently complex, for change to be traumatic. No doubt for many data processing managers it was impossible to imagine entering other supply relationships. Such links are reinforced by the strength of long-established personal ties between strategically placed individuals in buyer and supplier. No doubt many similar relationships will continue in existence: not necessarily the most 'efficient', but perhaps the least bad for many users. Indeed the new Information Services manager at AS recognised the implications of moving to a new supplier portfolio too quickly and sought to deal, as part of the new senior management team, with the planned organisational changes first, before introducing a new IT base and a new balance between internal and external expertise.

There are few comfortably symmetrical propositions to be made about the user–supplier relationship other than the conclusion drawn from our TE case study that mechanistic users and collaboratively inclined suppliers do not mix. Nevertheless, for firms looking to supply chain relationships to improve internal cost control and quality, getting value for money from the expertise of suppliers and customers is vital. From the point of view of users, whether or not suppliers are straightforwardly collaborative makes little difference. What sets the balance of power between users and suppliers is the market context against which transactions take place, where the most important variables are the size of the user, and hence the volume of potential custom it represents, and the nature of the technology and how much competitive edge it affords. In the final analysis, the relationship is inherently mixed motive: its value on either side will consequently depend in part on the skill of respective negotiators in injecting substantive content in the form of expertise which goes beyond the exchange of money for equipment.

7 Organisational change and expert managing

SOCIAL CONSTRUCTION AS A CATALYST OF ORGANISATIONAL CHANGE

In the last four chapters we have seen in some detail how companies have defined and managed expertise, and traced out some of the organisational consequences. However, interesting though case studies can be, without a theoretical framework they are no more than a number of scenes unconnected by a plot. Underlying all the organisational issues we have examined is the question of how to generalise: how can we move from the empirical detail of product development in Midas or sales strategies at Telewave Electronics (TE) to say something meaningful about technology, relationships between companies and the management of expertise in the computer systems sector as a whole? Beyond that, since questions about the management of expertise are not restricted to the sector, or even to private sector industry, we ought to be able to draw conclusions relevant to the study of organisations in general. A book solely about the management of expertise and the supply chain in companies dealing in computer technologies would be of interest to a wide spread of people, but it would still be a book written for too narrow an audience.

In making sense of the empirical material presented in the preceding chapters, we need to use our knowledge of the companies which figure in the case studies and the technologies they are involved in, as a point of departure from which we can address wider questions of the nature of organisational change, the role which technology, experts and managers play in it, and what can be said to underlie and direct it. In doing so, we will be arguing that much current theorising about business organisation is inadequate, because it ignores non-economic determinants of organisational structure. Or, to put it in less jargon-ridden terms, organisational change is a much more complicated and interesting process than commonly imagined by economists, because it is often precipitated not by economic factors but by the ideas strategically placed people have in their heads. It is not a complicated process: senior managers have an image of the ideal type of organisation which they would like their company to become. They generally think in terms of a continuum, with their ideal at one end and its opposite at the other, along which they locate the present structure of their company. The ideal is, in effect, a blueprint for organisational change. The way experts and expertise are managed, what types of technologies are acquired, through what types of relationship with other companies – all these can be wholly or partly determined by the image of the ideal organisation in the heads of senior managers.

The image of the ideal organisation varies, but does so in systematic ways, because it is an image that, like notions of expertise, is socially constructed. One method of dissecting the way something is socially constructed is to look at the categories being used to define and order perceived reality. There is a large body of social science which does precisely this, and which has established that much social construction is organised along dualisms, linked but opposing categories which are effectively mirror images of each other. These dualisms can be thought of as the building blocks of a system of classification, since that is what they ultimately become. The system of organisational classification works, like other classificatory systems, by setting up two model organisations, one at each end of the spectrum, which are structurally opposed. The spectrum then becomes a kind of mental map, and certain organisational attributes are taken to reveal where, along the continuum, a particular organisation is located, and in what direction organisational change is proceeding. Far from being solely an abstract concept, such a classificatory system also becomes a catalyst of social change. People become committed to one of the two organisational ideals, which necessarily means opposing the other. One or other ideal may be held up as desirable by managers, workers, politicians or academics, and actively promoted by policy or business texts. It becomes a model which is consciously worked towards. One or other end of the spectrum becomes invested with moral, economic and political values: it may be defined as more desirable, more just, more profitable, more appropriate to a particular market, and so forth. It will even underlie the language and metaphors people use to describe organisations.

We aim to examine the dualisms underlying the social construction of organisational change, and show how classifying organisations in certain ways leads in short order to very concrete decisions about what technologies to acquire and how to deal with supply chain relationships. We present a structuralist analysis of a system of organisational classification, and argue that this system underlies and shapes a significant portion of business life: it also has ramifications that go well beyond the computer industry.

However, the fact that we focus on social construction rather than economic variables does not mean we are arguing that business life is in the final analysis to do with culture or social psychology rather than economics: that would merely replace economic determinism by something equally unsustainable. Our argument is that the analysis of organisational change has in the past been handicapped by over-deterministic arguments. In seeking a unitary explanation of complex processes, these invariably come up with generalising models that aim to bludgeon the empirical into shape rather than analyse it properly. It is no part of our intention to replace economic determinism by any other form of determinism.

It is self-evident that the economic environment a firm operates within can shape its organisational form: recessions involve cutbacks in labour forces and less investment in new technologies, to take one obvious example. What we are arguing is that the orthodox explanations for organisational change at the level of the firm, and relationships between firms, are too simplistic. If one had to make a single generalisation about the mass of organisational research in the academic and business literature, it would be that it seeks to link economic factors directly to organisational structure. Burns and Stalker, for example, after defining the distinction between mechanistic and organic companies, suggested that mechanistic companies were appropriate to stable markets with low levels of innovation and organic companies would fit with highly innovatory, unstable markets. Organisational change, in effect, is conceptualised as the result of the relationship between a firm and its market environment: disjunctions between a firm's structure and its ability to respond to the demands of the marketplace are perceived by management, and structural changes are made – which may or may not succeed, as they also precipitate stresses within firms. The economic environment, in other words, functions rather as the natural environment in the theory of evolution: structural changes are made in organisations as they attempt to adapt to it, and the 'fittest' survive. Indeed, whenever recession strikes in Britain and the USA, Darwinian metaphors of natural selection are frequently used by governments and business people to rationalise rising unemployment, with electorates assured that those going to the wall are the brontosauri of the business world and the companies that survive, 'leaner and fitter', will be well placed to exploit their niches in the post-recessionary economic ecosystem.

But this type of analysis is only ever half – and sometimes not even that – of the real story. The images which people construct of their organisation, the typologies they build up of other organisations, the attributes which are ascribed to particular groups within organisations, the conceptions of desirable and undesirable change, the defining of certain actions as dangerous and others as safe, notions of effective and ineffective organisation structures, the labelling of certain organisational features as modern and others as outdated – all of these directly affect the nature and direction of organisational change, because they are part of the ideological charter underlying specific actions. Indeed much current business school theory, management consultancy and at least some management practice has defined a particular organisational model as the one best suited to obtaining competitive advantage. This has itself become an important catalyst of organisational change, even in the absence of the kind of technical innovations, market changes or other economic variables assumed by economists and others to be the real driving force of restructuring. The restructuring of AS, after its takeover by Corporate Booze, occurred without any significant changes in its economic environment either before or after, it will be remembered. According to corporate management, recession has, if anything, strengthened the direction of changes already under way, with continuing investment in technology and associated reorganisation of packaging and bottling causing job losses as production is 'rationalised'. Economic variables, in other words, are not the only kind of variables capable of provoking organisational changes. When they are a factor they do not act directly upon the firm, but are first passed through the reflecting – and distorting – prism of social construction.

Abstract though parts of this argument have been, the end product is very concrete. What it boils down to is fairly simple. Theories of organisational change have to be anchored in the empirical; in a study of the computer industry, this means in the patterns of business transactions and company organisation of the sector. What shapes actions in the business world and its institutions is the interplay between economic environment and social construction. It follows that neither should be given priority in the analysis of organisational structure and change. In one set of circumstances, say where high interest rates provoke a liquidity crisis which forces dismissals, economic context is clearly the driving factor. In another set of circumstances, say where the senior management of Corporate Booze have very strong ideas about how they can increase profitability in AS, social construction – in this case, the forging of a model of business organisation and the defining of it as 'better' – predominates. In most cases, both social construction and economics will be at work. Organisational change, it follows, is neither economically nor culturally determined, but patterned by both. Which of the two, if either, is more important in a given case is something that can only be decided by an analysis which takes both into account.

We also need to clarify what we mean by 'organisational change', and consider how it fits into the analytical framework outlined above. Organisational change is best thought of as proceeding along three axes and in two dimensions. It is not only a question of structural alterations in institutional form, like the formation of a combined marketing and sales department in a company where they had been separated or the setting up of a new government agency responsible for environmental matters. It also embraces the social relationships and work practices within an organisation. Finally, it includes the relationships between organisations: these are economic and/or institutional in nature, as in a contractual agreement, but necessarily involve relationships between people who work in separate organisations.

All three of these axes exist in two dimensions, the formal and informal. The distinction between the formal and informal is central to ethnography, and it was our firm belief that it was both under-represented and underestimated in the research literature about business that led to our decision to use ethnographic methodologies. As the material we have presented in the preceding chapters shows, many of the relationships, work practices and procedures important to such vital areas for computer companies as product development, supply chain management and selling are tacit, unwritten, 'illegal', implicit, unintended – in short, informal. We saw how, for example, informal feedback loops were often more important in feeding back user experience into the product design cycle than formally institutionalised market research, and how different groups within a company will often contest notions of expertise handed down by senior management instead of working to them. Sometimes the informal dimension of organisation reinforces the formal dimension, but more often not: a notable feature of people in hierarchies, whether they are at the top, bottom or in the middle, is that they devote a considerable portion of their time to circumventing the institutions and procedures which are meant to direct their working lives.

This leads into a theoretical problem which has bedevilled much organisational research. The traditional model of organisational change in the business world, which treats it as the product of the economic environment acting upon company structure, fails to take into account the important role played by social construction. Ideas of organisational change that use the firm as a bounded unit of analysis, as Burns and Stalker did, are open to similar charges of being too simplistic, since they do not incorporate the complexity of the way in which firms in the real world actually operate. Burns and Stalker dealt with the internal workings of a number of electronics companies without taking into account the external relationships these companies had with other firms, most importantly suppliers and customers, and other relevant institutions, such as industry associations, regulatory and technical standards bodies and public sector institutions. But any company operates amid a tangled web of external relationships with other firms –

suppliers, customers, distributors, contractors, consultants and so forth – in an environment where technical standards have to be hammered out together with other manufacturers and national and international bureaucracies, where companies are subsumed by corporate takeovers and where new companies are regularly being formed by fission from established firms. It follows that any attempt to theorise organisational change needs to examine the extent to which these external relationships influence the internal workings of companies.

At the beginning of this chapter, we raised the problem of how we can generalise from individual case studies. The answer, which the rest of the chapter will be devoted to demonstrating, is that the common thread underlying the case study material is a particular form of social construction, built on dualisms. Although cast as images of ideal organisations – which necessarily include both the utopian and dystopian, since ideal categories are only meaningful in relation to their opposites – they are not about specific firms, but are about a complex of personal and institutional relationships, both internal and external to the firm. These relationships are not solely economic in nature, despite their origin in the workplace. They do not just include the obvious issues of work organisation, power, authority and status central to much organisational research. Most importantly, the model we present here is also about how people conceptualise organisations and organisational change.

THE MODEL ORGANISATION: THE TECHNICAL ENTREPRENEURIAL SPECTRUM

Most analysis of organisations and organisational change takes place outside universities. The exact number of students of organisational behaviour is unknown but can be numbered in the hundreds of thousands, perhaps even in millions. Both these assertions may seem surprising, but consider for a moment what large sections of the population in any advanced industrial economy do for a living.

Few researchers have such intense and protracted involvement with the communities they study as most people have with their own, or other, organisations. Salespeople are good examples of applied researchers of organisations. In a large computer systems supplier, as we have seen, many members of a salesforce may have worked on a particular customer account for many years. They develop a deep intimacy with their target company, poring over its accounts and making projections of turnover, observing people moving into and out of jobs, and charting structural change within the company. They do this because success in their own job depends on being able to make finely nuanced judgements about events in the customer firm.

Salespeople who fail to analyse acquisitions procedures correctly, or who wrongly identify who has the power to sign cheques, are not likely to survive for very long. Unlike academic researchers, none of them, even those working on a single company account for years at a time, would make the mistake of seeing 'their' firm as a bounded unit of analysis. They know that customers are part of regional, national and international economies, a component of industrial sectors that wax and wane according to a number of economic variables – and also social ones, since demand for products is in part socially patterned, as demonstrated by the rise in demand for, say, lead-free petrol. It is a vital part of salespeoples' jobs to make sophisticated judgements about economic change and its implications for their target firms over time. This necessarily involves classifying the companies they are selling to, and plotting the axes of structural change within them.

Middle and senior managers can be thought of as students of organisational behaviour in the same way. Managers can take different attitudes to restructuring, but whether they choose to advance it, obstruct it or remain indifferent to it, they still need conceptions of the past, present and future nature of the organisation, and the roles they have played and will play within it. They make assessments of market conditions and plan organisational responses. They read management textbooks, go to industry seminars and trade fairs, do courses in business schools, and are generally bombarded with a variety of received wisdoms about good and bad practice. All of this involves the modelling of organisations, literally and meta-phorically. Managers are paid to have ideas about diagnosing problems and improving performance. But in order to think as managers, they need to select certain organisational characteristics and use them as a basis for classifying and categorising. This classification takes the form, as we have argued, of an ideological spectrum with the utopian organisation at one end and the dystopian organisation at the other. An organisation is categorised in terms of the spectrum, and organisational change is conceived of as movement along it, in either direction. The direction of change, and whether managers regard it as desirable or not, is at least in the abstract entirely relative: one manager's utopia may be another's dystopia, and many conflicts can be reduced to the clash between opposing definitions of the ideal organisation.

We have called the ideological spectrum which was underlying our informants' conceptions of organisational change the technical–entrepreneurial spectrum. We have called the ideal types at either end of the axis the technical and the entrepreneurial organisation, the basic features of which are mapped out in Figure 3. The spectrum is formed by a number of dualisms, which together form a classificatory system. As was the case with Burns and Stalker's concepts of organic and mechanistic companies, the entrepreneurial organisation and the technical organisation represent ideal-ised types rather than real organisations; they are striven for rather than achieved.

Which end of the spectrum is selected as the ideal in any given case – or, to put it another way, which direction of movement along the axis is defined as desirable – is essentially a political question. It revolves around the distribution of power in organisations, and how effectively it is wielded. It involves the power to impose a direction on events within the organisation, the power to overcome internal resistance and the capacity to forge the kind of external relationships with other organisations which further the desired internal changes. The technologies used within the organisation, and particularly the computer systems so crucial to information flows within it, inevitably become one of the fields where battle is joined between those who

	Technical	Entrepreneurial
Management structure	Hierarchical Decentralised Autonomous departments	Hierarchical Centralised Corporate control
Work relations	Authoritarian Rigid job boundaries High segmentation Class-ridden	Egalitarian Fluid job boundaries Low segmentation Meritocratic
Supply chain relationships	Stable Inertial Collaboration Low competition Institutionalised cost control	Unstable Confrontational 'Strategic' collaboration High competition Price/quality comparison institutionalised
Technical policy	Aspires to technical autonomy High internal technical capacity Function prime factor in technology acquisition	Contracts out many technical functions Internal targeted technical capacity Compatibility prime factor in technology acquisition
Management of expertise	Segregated 'Techie' 'Scientist' Specialist	Integrated Hybrid technologist/ manager Provider of business service Generalist

Figure 3 The technical–entrepreneurial spectrum

wish to push the organisation towards either end of the spectrum. Because technology in general, and information systems in particular, have profound implications for the balance of power and the exercise of managerial authority within the organisation, the management of experts and expertise is a key issue in organisational politics. The technical–entrepreneurial spectrum is therefore more explicitly expressed at senior levels of management hierarchies, where the exercise of power and the control of organisational change are part of formal job remits.

The technical–entrepreneurial spectrum takes in five key organisational variables. These did not come from a theoretical model set up before fieldwork began, but reflect the importance given to certain organisational features by our informants. The spectrum can be classed as grounded theory. It is possible to argue that as we were concentrating specifically on questions related to the management of expertise, a different focus of interest might have led to different organisational criteria being used as the raw material for social construction. However, with the possible exception of the category specifically about the management of expertise, which reflects the initial analytical focus of our research, the other categories relate to organisational change in general. Before we look at the set of dualisms that make up the classificatory system, however, we need to make clear precisely what the scope of the technical–entrepreneurial spectrum is.

The first and most important point to make is that it is a taxonomy of organisations which operate in markets. As such, it embraces both public and private sector organisations, encompassing private sector companies, privatised utilities and public sector bodies being forced into some form of market participation, even if it is an internal market such as that created by the 1980s reforms to the British National Health Service. The spectrum reflects the priorities of informants, for whom the categorising of organisations was a central part of work routines, both to assess the progress (or lack) of change in their own firm, and as a basis for formulating strategies to deal with other organisations. For researchers, it has the advantage of being a qualitative scale which can be used to classify organisations. For policymakers and other interested parties, it offers an insight into the way managers and experts conceive of organisational change and the role new technologies are intended to play in it, which in turn feeds directly into the design, selling and implementation of computer equipment and systems.

Second we were often struck during the course of fieldwork at the way informants homed in upon the nature of work relations as one of the main criteria for distinguishing between organisations. This was especially marked in TE, which has a North American company ethos stressing openness, managerial accessibility and collaboration between workforce and management. Everyone made a point of being on first-name terms with everyone else, for example, and lapel badges were provided to make this possible. Nothing could have contrasted more markedly with one of its British customers, Defence Electronics, where the single TE canteen was replaced by a complex hierarchy of eating places restricted to certain employee grades. In our case study firms, the organisation of work was assumed to flow from corporate culture, management style or 'our way of doing things', common phrases which are synonyms for dominant ideologies about the nature of relationships within the firm. The way employees classify work relations within the firm necessarily involves dealing with the question of power, how it is exercised and how it is represented, all of which determine the organisation of the workplace. Socially constructing the workplace, in other words, is an inherently political process. It is therefore inevitable that a central element in the technical–entrepreneurial spectrum has to do with classifying the social organisation of production. This reflects the importance given to this dimension of organisational life by those we interviewed, but also the more general point that no classification system will have much meaning unless it deals with power relationships arising from the workplace.

Finally the technical–entrepreneurial spectrum is predictive: it can be used as the basis for generalisations about organisational structures and external relationships. First the variables which make up each side of the spectrum are linked: movement towards one end of the spectrum in one variable implies movement in others. Thus, for example, a move towards centralising managerial authority will be associated with, amongst other things, a switch away from function towards compatibility as the main criterion of computer systems acquisition, and a more active, potentially confrontational approach towards the management of suppliers. Where apparent anomalies occur, for example when a company with a management structure inclining towards the technical has work relations more characteristic of the entrepreneurial organisation, this leads to stresses as the organisation is pulled both ways. These anomalous situations may occur as a result of struggles over the direction of change, with different interest groups seeking to mould the parts of the organisation which they effectively control in the favoured direction. Should these anomalies persist, however, the lack of clear direction is likely to inhibit organisational performance. This explains why so many attempts to restructure organisations – in other words, push them towards one end of the spectrum – do not succeed: the transitional period where the organisation is pulled both ways lasts too long, workforce and management become confused and demoralised, and performance collapses.

The rest of this section will take the form of a discussion of each of the five defining variables of the technical and entrepreneurial spectrum laid out in Figure 3.

Management structure

The exercise of authority within firms is by definition hierarchical, but there are a wide variety of ways in which managements may attempt to exert it. Some firms have a management hierarchy that is explicitly thought of as a pyramid: others have several distinct centres of authority. Struggles between contending centres of authority invariably underpin conflicts at the managerial level. The problem is particularly acute for large organisations whose ambit is either national or international rather than regional. They face obvious problems of co-ordination, but they also have to face the further issue of how to organise the distribution of authority in a structure where change is often continuous. Large private sector firms, for example, are typically made up of a number of geographically separated plants which may be serving different markets and dealing with different suppliers. They have their own internal sectional interests to pursue over issues like allocation of investment, level and patterns of recruitment, equipment acquisition, operational budgets and performance targets, to name only the most obvious. A similar observation could be made of many national and international agencies in the public sector. The distribution of power and authority between the component parts of the organisation is thus centrally important for managers. How managerial structures develop to enable the exercise of power is one of the main criteria people use to differentiate between organisations. Simply put, what it reduces to is how much autonomy the component parts of the organisation have.

Both the technical and the entrepreneurial organisation have a hierarchical management structure: they are not collectives and authority is not highly devolved down the hierarchy. The difference between them centres around two factors. The first is the degree to which authority is centralised. The second is the relationship between departments and the theoretical central locus of authority: the board, managing directors, steering committee, a government minister, chief executives or, the all-embracing word used by TE managers to refer to central authority in general, 'corporate'.

In the technical organisation, the hierarchy is generally steeper and more complicated; in practice authority is dispersed. Departments may become a law unto themselves, and departmental managers have considerable autonomy to make their own decisions on internal issues, like recruitment, purchasing and work organisation. The company as a whole is a confederation of departmental empires, and empire-building explicitly or implicitly, is, the dominant motive behind the actions of heads of department. While this generates problems, there are compensating advantages. There are two main problems. The first is that the lack of co-ordination combines with the minimal flow of information between departments to produce a lack of standardisation in work practices, and therefore the inefficient use of resources. It might mean for example that research laboratories in different parts of the organisation are working in isolation on problems which ideally need the synergy of multidisciplinary co-operation. For ICI to produce a new variety of pest-resistant seed, for example, it needs separate biotechnology, agronomy and pharmaceuticals laboratories to work together. This degree of interdependence implies a high level of centralised managerial control if it is to work. The second problem typically generated by the management structure of the technical organisation is the contentious nature of policymaking and decision-making at senior management level. Instead of an agreed central authority with its writ running through all levels and implemented by departments, a number of departmental emperors use their relative autonomy and their departmental fiefdoms to press for more influence and resourses at corporate level, rather as medieval European monarchies were plagued by unruly barons.

On the other hand, the way technical organisations are managed has the advantage of being popular with many people who work within them, especially experts. They may be paternalistic, with senior and junior management linked by a network of clientelistic ties. Supervision becomes relaxed and little attempt is made to monitor job performance intensively. This is hardly surprising: a decentralised management structure which devolves power to heads of departments gives them considerable powers of patronage, and a large clientele is necessary to serve as a regional power base to departmental barons pressing their case for additional resources. Technical organisations are frequently popular with experts, since the structure is suited to providing them with both the resources and the freedom they regard as necessary to creativity and innovation. Technical organisations tend to subscribe to the widely accepted social constructions of expertise outlined in Chapter 2 of the expert as privileged possessor of specialised knowledge. The R&D department may therefore approximate towards the stereotypical academic model, being left to get on with it and not closely supervised by profit-oriented managers. It will tend to value innovation *per se* rather than see it first and foremost as a means to generate profit. The technical company in a high-technology sector tends to innovate first and then think about the market for the new product afterwards. They think of themselves as engineering companies, and their managers admit that they have always been weaker in anything to do with marketing.

Where the technical organisation is a loose federation of departments, the entrepreneurial organisation centralises power at corporate level and simplifies and flattens the hierarchy, eliminating middle management. With this simpler structure, the component parts of the firm are kept under tight control, and centralised management authority functions as the leash. Whatever the rhetoric, the structure of the entrepreneurial organisation is about policing and supervision; allowing organisational space to any group other than senior managers is anathema to its philosophy. Relative autonomy of action is deliberately negotiated with a particular group and is carefully circumscribed. Departmental managers are allowed as little autonomy as practicable, and corporate spends a great deal of time ensuring that departments work together rather than against each other. From being departmental emperors in a technical organisation, managers always have corporate looking over their shoulder, monitoring job and business performance and intervening immediately if problems are perceived. Entrepreneurial organisations are not always popular with people who work in them. During periods of restructuring they almost always have staff turnover rates considerably higher than those found in technical organisations. It is thus a particularly traumatic experience for employees when an entrepreneurial organisation takes over a technical one and tries to mould it in its own image: the case of the takeover of AS by Corporate Booze will be remembered, where many managers and experts, committed to the organisational ideal of the technical company, voted with their feet. Problems of consent to authority are dealt with by the creation of a corporate ethos or ideology which encourages identification with the goals of corporate management and seeks to persuade the workforce that their individual well-being can be equated with the objectives of corporate growth. Reward and appraisal systems have to be brought into line to reinforce the desired performance.

Work relations

In terms of organisational theory, work relations in the technical company are similar to Burns and Stalker's mechanistic firm, and could be traced back to Weber's notion of a segmented, hierarchical bureaucracy (Weber, 1948). They are characterised by a highly differentiated and relatively stable occupational hierarchy. Flexibility is not a word often heard: occupations have defined boundaries around them. An extreme example of the highly differentiated occupational structure typical of the technical organisation would be the guild-like organisation of British newspaper publishing before the changes of the 1980s. Unions were able to institutionalise a highly segmented system where each job had its parameters exhaustively defined. Work was divided up and allocated between jobs, with an absolute prohibition against one type of worker performing any part of the function allocated to another. A social scientist would describe the work relations of the technical organisation as characterised by a high degree of functional segmentation – people are assigned their occupational roles, with or without negotiating them beforehand, and then stick to them. A mistake it is important not to fall into here is thinking of work relations in the technical organisation as somehow more structured than in the entrepreneurial organisation. The implicit assumption that there are organisations where work relations are unstructured, or less structured, is misleading. The contrast between work relations in the entrepreneurial and the technical organisation has nothing to do with the degree of structure: the web of social relationships which arise out of the workplace may be more informal in the entrepreneurial organisation, but it is no less structured for that.

The form work relations assume in the entrepreneurial organisation is governed by the absolute priority afforded to flexibility, the most obviously socially constructed term in the contemporary organisational lexicon. Workers and managers are encouraged not to let outmoded concepts like formal job remits, occupational boundaries and segmentation get in the way of improving performance and generating profit. Performance is continuously monitored, using the centralised management structure and the information channelled directly to corporate by the type of IT network most favoured by entrepreneurial organisations: integrated across the organisation and linked directly to senior management. Any filtering by remaining middle managers is avoided. While performance may indeed improve, measured in terms of productivity and profits, the strategy also has costs. Work in the entrepreneurial organisation creates unlimited liabilities for the managers and workers, in the same way as it did for the organic company manager, and not everyone is prepared to allow work to take such a central place in their lives. A characteristic of many ex-technical organisations being pushed towards the entrepreneurial model is that higher staff turnover becomes institutionalised in the shape of a continuing proportion of short-term contracts. In the private sector, entrepreneurial organisations are attracted by philosophies which stress continuous change and improvement, such as total quality management and just-in-time. The workplace in the entrepreneurial firm tends to be festooned with charts recording individual and departmental productivity.

The more a company inclines towards either end of the spectrum, the more authoritarian social relations within it become, although the form authoritarianism assumes is different. In the technical organisation, highly layered and segmented, each organisational level has clearly defined relations of dominance and subordination with layers above and below, rather as in a military rank system. Thus they tend to have promotion and salary systems based on seniority and formal qualifications, as well as job performance. These ascriptive practices are regarded with horror inside the entrepreneurial organisation, which has an egalitarian 'corporate culture'.

Promotion and salary is based, at least theoretically, on assessments of merit alone. Yet this egalitarianism is combined, as we have seen, with a centralising management structure which concentrates power at corporate level rather than distributing it to departments, and with close monitoring of job performance.

Supply chain relationships

The way organisations manage supply chain relationships is often vital to their performance: commercial success increasingly depends not just on having a good product, but on the successful negotiation of transactions with suppliers, customers and distributors.

Of all the external relationships entered into, it is the way that a company manages supplier relationships which is the surest clue to where it should be placed along the technical–entrepreneurial spectrum. The technical organis- ation is likely to adopt a *laissez-faire* or inertial collaborative approach to suppliers, for a number of reasons. Technical organisations are compara- tively conservative, opting for low-risk strategies to manage uncertainty: they do not have the organisational flexibility that is deliberately cultivated by the entrepreneurial organisation, and consequently tend to stick with a supplier they consider adequate. They have frequently operated in stable markets for many years, where the supply chain holds few surprises. Change may be regarded as too much effort for too little reward. In addition, delimited job boundaries and relatively low staff mobility encourage the formation of long-term informal ties between supplier and user personnel which cement the institutional relationship. They may even contribute to improving product development in the supplier, since informal feedback loops flourish best in a relatively stable institutional setting. Cost control is likely to be the official goal of supply chain management and this is generally institutionalised in the form of a specialist purchasing function, rewarded for price control or cost-cutting. However, as we have seen, the espoused objective may be subverted by internal technical experts working informally with a preferred supplier to ensure that 'their' supplier gets the contract. Separation between purchasing, rewarded for performance on cost, and engineering, engaged in long-term dialogue with peers in suppliers, puts the emphasis on internal bargaining between functions over the acquisition of new technology. Suppliers respond by trying to use internal engineering functions as their agents.

The entrepreneurial organisation, in contrast, will adopt a more explicitly confrontational approach. It may favour 'management by terror', keeping supplier options as open as possible. It chooses to make suppliers compete against each other for 'authorised vendor status', and has no compunction in switching suppliers if their terms change. As a result, it tends to have several supplier relationships in strategic areas at any one time, and regards the inertial approach of the technical organisation as commercially foolish. As a matter of policy entrepreneurial organisations avoid becoming deeply committed to a supplier, and when they are forced into monogamy, as happens when there is no alternative source of supply for a technology, managers worry about over-dependence. In sum, supplier relationships in the technical organisation tend to be collaborative and long term, and the level of competition between suppliers is low. In the entrepreneurial organisation, there is active competition between suppliers, and supplier–user relationships are likely to be more confrontational, with the espoused 'strategic partnership' model emphasising the need to improve quality as well as controlling costs. The presence of a collaborative element in such transactions depends on the ability of the buyer to work with the supplier, for example to use the supplier's expertise to implement a new computer system or conversely to invest engineering effort to improve the supplier's product quality.

Technical policy

One of the main reasons for choosing the word technical to describe one end of the spectrum is the attitude and policies certain organisations have towards technology and technical work. The importance of this issue for the management of organisations has increased steadily with the growing sophistication of computer systems. The technical organisation, as its name suggests, places a great deal of stress on its technical capabilities. Expanding its internal skills base is a priority. Although in practice not even the largest multinational can be fully technically autonomous, the technical organisation attempts to be autonomous in specialised knowledge, skills and personnel. Within technical organisations, prestige is measured by the extent to which a department engages in technically complex work. R&D departments tend to carry the most internal clout, expressed concretely in the size of budgets and salaries and symbolically in a value system and status hierarchy that grants special privileges and autonomy to the expert. Research scientists working in product development, for example, are allowed a latitude in dress, work routines and relations with superiors which would be unthinkable for other categories of employee. Indeed, the more socially inept the research scientist is, the better a certain type of manager is pleased, saying with pride to visitors how 'we have some people we would never let the customer see': management does what it can, genius does what it must.

The high value placed on technical autonomy has important implications for the way in which the acquisition of new technology is managed. Technology purchases will usually be steered through by engineers in the semi-independent departmental structure typical of the technical organisation. Engineers make the decisions and managers accept that equipment acquisition is a job to be left to the 'experts'. Provided the cheque is not too outrageous, managers will sign it. The most important criterion for the acquisition will be function, not compatibility. Strategic considerations, such as the place any individual acquisition should have in the wider purchasing priorities of the organisation, tend not to enter into the equation. The drive to increase in-house technical capabilities, combined with the tendency to dream about capacity rather than think about applications (a possible consequence of the overwhelming domination of the engineering profession by men), often results in technical purchases being both over-priced and incompatible with existing technology.

Managers in entrepreneurial organisations, of course, love to tell horror stories about technology acquisitions by technical organisations. Such managers regard particular forms of information and communication technologies as important instruments of organisational change. Their ideal organisation is tightly controlled from the centre. As a result, managers place great stress on monitoring performance, and for them no issue is more important than assuring smooth flows of information between all levels of the organisation. Computer systems therefore present themselves as strategic aids which enable any separatist tendencies in recalcitrant parts of the company to be monitored and controlled. With close monitoring of all relevant details of production processes and performance, it becomes much more difficult for departments to maintain independence and more strategic attitudes towards purchasing can be enforced. There is especially tight central control of IT purchasing, given its strategic potential. Technical experts are involved in the purchasing process, but in a team with other business managers, to provide the information needed about compatibility with existing systems and technical performance. The relationships between systems rather than absolute technical merits become the prime consideration in the decision to purchase, with function inevitably losing out to compatibility.

The management of expertise

One word frequently heard in both entrepreneurial and technical organis-ations is 'techie', a slang term meaning a technologist or technical expert. Its connotations vary revealingly depending on context: in a technical organisation it is a simple descriptive term, but in an entrepreneurial organisation it is more usually an insult, at best an ironic tag. The way firms define and deal with experts is closely linked to their technical policy. The traditional 'man in the white coat' stereotype of the expert is associated with technical organisations: experts are a highly visible professional caste, segregated from other types of employee and capable of working as a cohesive interest group against business managers in certain situations. The entrepreneurial organisation, in contrast, favours integration over segregation. A conscious effort is made to ensure that a 'techie' constituency never forms. Those who have specialised knowledge are expected to subordinate the accumulation and perfecting of that knowledge to thinking about applications and markets, and the deployment of their expertise to generate profit. The dominant image of the expert is not the traditional scientist but the member of a project team, the supplier of a business service together with colleagues.

This has direct implications for managerial attitudes towards the knowledge and skills base within organisations. Everything in the technical organisation is geared towards developing specialisation and cultivating scientific and engineering expertise. In the entrepreneurial organisation, the social construction of expertise redefines it in more broadly based terms, combining specialised technical knowledge with an emphasis on applications, specialised managerial knowledge and business performance. This in turn has implications for the management of supply chain relationships. Entrepreneurial organisations will contract out many technical functions. What technical specialisation there is will be highly targeted on the skills and technologies identified as most important to business performance. This is another factor which pushes entrepreneurial organisations to enter into 'strategic partnerships'.

INTER-FIRM RELATIONSHIPS AND ORGANISATIONAL STRUCTURES: A CONCEPTUAL FRAMEWORK

The above discussion of ideal types has led us to revise our starting point, which expressed change along two dimensions: first, organisational types and second, inter-organisational relationships, and to suggest a simple two-way conceptual model which depicts, in idealised form, the nature of contemporary debate about organisational restructuring and the supply chain (Figure 4).

In theory, the entrepreneurial form is meant to be associated with a more interventionist management of supply chain relationships: the traditional distributive, price-led bargain is replaced by integrative negotiation, which seeks to maximise joint profit through 'strategic partnerships' (see, for example, Carlisle and Parker, 1989). We have argued that such 'partnerships' are not a guarantee of integrative bargains, however, and can, on the contrary, be a label for a variety of different relationships, from highly

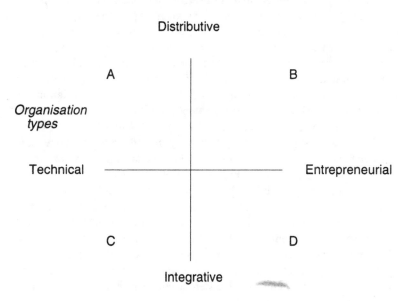

Figure 4 Organisational types and inter-firm relationships

confrontational, distributive bargains to genuine attempts at integrative solutions. During periods of economic recession, 'partnership' can simply be a word used by larger firms to impose terms on small suppliers, increasingly desperate for orders.

Our two-way model results in four quadrants, and forces us to think about the implications of a number of permutations and combinations of structures and inter-firm relationships. In principle, any firm could be located in one of the four quadrants. Quadrant A would contain the bureaucratic hierarchical organisations which have clearly defined rules and regulations governing customer–supplier relations. One example of such large organisations are the local authorities, responsible for massive sums of public money, and hence needing structures for public accountability. Suppliers tender for contracts according to formal specifications, and at the end of the day price is the remaining uncertainty. This approach may work efficiently enough as long as the organisation has its own skilled people, able to generate an appropriate system specification. Internal bargaining between interest groups may nevertheless play an important part in the final outcome, and there is limited internal capacity for handling acquisitions when the potential applications of the technology are uncertain. Firms in quadrant B would be responsive to changing market demands for their products or services and would for example be concerned to investigate the benefits of new technologies; their internal structures may be in a state of flux, but they would nevertheless continue to adopt a distributive approach to customer–supplier relations. In our case studies, Midas provided an example of this type of firm. In contrast, those in quadrant C would recognise the importance of establishing closer links with their suppliers and yet their internal division of labour and management system would be formalised and bureaucratic. Inertial forms of collaboration, such as those observed in Defence Electronics (DE), may dominate supplier–user links. The final quadrant D would be occupied by firms who operate with the entrepreneurial system of management and also aim to establish active 'integrative' supply chain relationships. Arguably both Telewave Electronics and AS fall into this category, although Albion IT systems managers espoused the benefits of a more confrontational approach to suppliers than TE managers, whose preferred language was one of collaboration, reflecting their different company ethos, but also their different market situations.

Perhaps the main value of two-way categorisation is that it alerts us to some of the contradictions inherent in the current debates about entrepreneurial structures and supplier–user relationships. In reality organisations and their external relationships do not fit easily into categories. Aspects of both structures continue to coexist within firms and, as our case studies have shown, supply relationships are inherently mixed motive: there is always the potential for one side to be massively exploited by the other, just as there is probably some potential in most transactions for some mutual gain. The outcome depends on the ability of the negotiators to control the conflictual aspects of the transaction without damaging personal relationships between sides. There are a variety of ways to achieve this, including the use of specialised negotiators at different stages of the contract. We saw one example of an evolving division of labour in the case of Telewave Electronics managing computer systems sales.

The main difficulty to be faced by senior management, however, is the tension, if not direct contradiction, between the need for expertise and the need for co-ordination and acceptance of authority. Contemporary concern with product quality is resulting in greater emphasis on the development of expertise, and the use of discretion, at all levels of the workforce. Yet this sits uneasily with a command mentality on the part of management. It is this crisis which 'new' organisational forms are meant to address, with project teams and 'hybrid' manager–experts used to tie lower levels of the work-force into senior management objectives. Concerns about authority and co-ordination remain unresolved, however: the orientation to the customer gives weight to the need for expertise by the principal occupants of boundary roles, but also sharpens the employer's need to instill a sense of loyalty rather than simple adherence to the rules. It was clear from our case study firms that there was no easy resolution of this problem. If people are expected to use their intelligence in one sphere of their work, they expect a greater say in others, and expect the rewards to be greater. Hence in the idealised entrepreneurial firm the reward for technical experts who relinquish their autonomy in the technical sphere is a greater role in business policy and an enhanced internal labour market, via the management hierarchy.

IMAGERY AND IMPLICATIONS OF THE TECHNICAL–ENTREPRENEURIAL SPECTRUM

There is no more complex topic in social science than the relationship between broad social and political changes and the emergence of the dualisms and categories which make up a system of classification. In the case of the technical–entrepreneurial spectrum analysis is complicated by the deep passions the discussion of organisations arouses. One thinks, for example, of the level of controversy that surrounds structural reform in the British National Health Service, with one side of the debate arguing that particular organisational forms designed to respond to market demand will deliver health care more efficiently, while the other argues that 'the market' is incompatible with the notion of care, since competition implies winners and losers. Ultimately, the spectrum cannot be divorced from wider economic, social and political change. In the USA, and even more markedly in many European countries, there has been a generalised shift over the past decade away from the technical towards the entrepreneurial organisation, in both ideological and empirical terms. This is to do with the 1980s dismantling of the corporatist mechanisms which insulated many organis-ations from the unimpeded action of markets. Such policy was a central part of the political programme of many governments. A more extreme example of the process is occurring in the 1990s in what used to be the Warsaw Pact countries, as those governments attempt to break with the organisational legacies of communism. The technical–entrepreneurial spectrum is not just a system of classification: it has become part of the complex of metaphors, images and ideologies swirling around the central political debate of the last thirty years – where the line between state regulation and the free operation of markets should be drawn.

One indication of the success achieved by those arguing for the sovereignty of the market is that the technical–entrepreneurial spectrum incorporates many of the ideological assumptions made by the New Right since the 1970s, which we can now say have passed out of the merely political to become part of popular culture. A particular type of organisation – hierarchical, inefficient, unresponsive, unsuccessful – is associated with the state and bureaucracy in general, while another type – flexible, efficient, egalitarian, successful – is associated with private sector industry and free markets. Since the 1970s, we would argue, amongst the key social constituency of senior managers and policymakers, and to a lesser extent amongst technical experts, the superiority of the entrepreneurial organisation has become accepted. Quite how this has come about would need a book to itself to be properly charted, but the broad outline of the process in Britain is clear. It had its origins in the 1970s in the widespread perception that the various corporatist mechanisms used to manage the economy and society had resulted in an economy that was visibly falling behind its European neighbours. Whether public disillusion provoked ideological attack or vice versa is a chicken and egg argument, but by the end of the 1970s it was certainly the case that powerful ideological attacks were being made on corporatism at precisely the time that the Left appeared to have run out of ideas. Central to this attack was hostility towards bureaucracy and the belief that it was the market, and being able to operate in markets, which was the key to efficient organisational structure. This then became the basis for the wide-ranging reforms after 1979, which were to a large extent the attempt to replace one type of organisation – traditional bureaucracy – with another, market-oriented and entrepreneurial. Interestingly, markets and the state were (and are) assumed to be more or less uniform in their respective action on organisational structure, which was in itself an indication of how politicised thinking about organisations has become. Equally, bureaucracy was assumed to be a much more monolithic organisational form than it actually is. Central to what became dominant ideology in the 1980s was a view of bureaucracy which saw it as the stratified, hierarchical and unresponsive offshoot of the state's expansion into new economic and social sectors.

To operate effectively in markets, dominant ideology states, you need to have an entrepreneurial organisation. Certain qualities are essential, notably the flexibility to facilitate a rapid response to external change, especially changes in demand. This organisational ideal was not arrived at through empirically based, deductive reasoning. Instead, as ideology tends to do, one true statement – that flexible organisational forms are best suited to settings where demand can change rapidly – was extended into the highly contentious generalisation that entrepreneurial organisations are *a priori* more efficient and effective than technical ones. It was noticeable that the managers, experts and policymakers we interviewed were using images and metaphors in a way that was not only meant to illustrate a point or make clear how something worked. They were also part of a symbolic vocabulary applied to organisations which were as much about passing judgement – and hence about approval and disapproval – as they were about description. Almost without exception, the entrepreneurial organisation would be identified with the future, and by extension modernity in general, and the technical by extension with the past, and implicitly with the outmoded. In a similar way, the entrepreneurial organisation would be identified with youth, and the physical connotations of youth were amongst the most common images used to portray organisations as they were or hoped to become: vigour, robustness, strength, health, quickness, resilience and so forth. This was opposed, explicitly or implicitly, to the identification of the technical organisation with old age and its associated physical problems: 'creaking at the joints', slow to react, etc. Approval and disapproval were symbolised by talking about organisations as if they were people, and people struggling to survive in a harsh environment at that, where youth and robustness was at a premium.

The images of time, the human body and the qualities associated with each end of the spectrum are sufficiently flexible, however, to be turned round with some slight differences of inflexion, so that the same or closely related images can have their meaning inverted. The result is to reverse the implicit moral framework so that the technical organisation is approved of and the entrepreneurial organisation despised. The images and metaphors people use to describe organisations, in other words, are double-edged. While youth serves as an image for healthy vigour and aggression, it also can be identified with rashness and instability: age can be an image for experience and solidity as well as frailty and inflexibility. During the 1980s dominant ideology has given firm approval to the entrepreneurial organisation. Not all markets reward flexible organisations, however, and some may even penalise them: there is a trade-off between flexibility and stability which works against entrepreneurial organisations in some settings, such as activities where careful long-term planning is necessary. However, social construction proceeds according to its own internal logic. The fact that selected aspects of certain types of market, and certain kinds of bureaucracy, were, at a given historical moment, taken as illustrating absolute truths about markets and organisations in general is what concerns us here. Whether the process was coherent or logically consistent is not as important as the fact that it happened and that it underlies what has become dominant organisational ideology, at least until culture and economics next combine to produce another upheaval in the patterns of social construction. It seems likely that in years to come a reaction is likely to occur, not least because of the negative impact of the entrepreneurial model on aspects of organisational life where the market has played little or no role in the past, such as the social organisation of health care and education. The technical–entrepreneurial spectrum should not be regarded as fixed or immutable: if we can plot its origins with a fair degree of confidence, it is possible to foresee its demise.

What then can we say of management and managers for the future? We have argued that there is 'no one best way', and no easy fit between an organisation's structure, its supply chain relationships and its economic environment. Even if there were such a functional prescription, the politics of organisational life would ensure that the blueprint would never be implemented in its absolute form. In an era when near monopolistic firms like IBM cannot get the formula right, the only safe conclusion is that the capacity of managers for critical reflection and redirection of organisations is at a premium. The challenge of the next decade is for the old-style functional managers and the traditional experts to demonstrate a new open-mindedness and to create the kinds of structures capable of combining the diffuse, practice-oriented expertise of managers with the abstract, ever-changing expertise of science and engineering.

References

Armstrong, P. (1984) 'Competition between the organisational professions and the evolution of management control strategies', in K. Thompson (ed.) *Work, Employment and Unemployment: Perspectives on Work and Society*, Milton Keynes: Open University Press.

Armstrong, P. (1989) 'Management, labour process and agency', *Work, Employment and Society*, 3, 307–22.

Burns, T. and Stalker, G. (1961) *The Management of Innovation*, London: Macmillan.

Burt, D.N. (1989) 'Managing suppliers up to speed', *Harvard Business Review*, 67, 127–35.

Carlisle, J.A. and Parker, R.C. (1989) *Beyond Negotiation: Redeeming Customer–Supplier Relationships*, Chichester: Wiley.

Clark, P. and Staunton, N. (1990) *Innovation in Technology and Organisation*, London: Routledge.

Cockburn, C. (1985) *Machinery of Dominance: Women, Men and Technical Know-How*, London: Pluto.

Dosi, G. (1984) *Technical Change and Industrial Transformation*, London: Macmillan.

Dyerson, R. and Roper, M. (1991) 'When expertise becomes know-how: the management of IT projects in financial services', London Business School: Technology Project Papers 11.

Fevre, R. (1987) 'Subcontracting in steel', *Work, Employment and Society*, 1, 509–27.

Fleck, J. (1988) 'Innofusion or diffusation?', Edinburgh University: PICT Working Paper 4.

Fleck, J. and Tierney, M. (1991) 'The management of expertise: knowledge, power and the economics of expert labour', Edinburgh University: PICT Working Paper 29.

Fleck, J, Webster, J and Williams, R. (1990) 'The dynamics of IT implementation: a reassessment of paradigms and trajectories of development', *Futures*, 22, 618–40.

Freeman, C. (1986) *Technology Policy and Economic Performance*, London: Pinter.

Friedman, A.L. and Cornford, D. (1989) *Computer Systems Development*, Chichester: Wiley.

Geertz, C. (1973) 'Thick description: towards an interpretive theory of culture', in C. Geertz (ed.) *The Interpretation of Cultures: Selected Essays*, New York: Basic Books.

Hamel, G. and Prahalad, C.K. (1989) 'Strategic intent', *Harvard Business Review*, 67, 63–76.

Hughes, E.C. (1971) *The Sociological Eye*, Chicago: Aldine Atherton.

Jaikumar, R. (1986) 'Post-industrial manufacturing', *Harvard Business Review*, 64, 69–76.

Kanter, R.M. (1989) 'The new managerial work', *Harvard Business Review*, 67, 85–92.

Morgan, G. (1988) *Riding the Waves of Change: Developing Managerial Competences for a Turbulent World*, London: Sage.

Morris, T. and Wood, S. (1991) 'Testing the survey method: continuity and change in British industrial relations', *Work, Employment and Society*, 5, 259–82.

Nelson, R. and Winter, S. (1982) *An Evolutionary Theory of Economic Change*, Cambridge, Mass.: Belknap Press.

Peters, T. (1987) *Thriving on Chaos*, Basingstoke: Macmillan.

Peters, T. (1991) 'The boundaries of business: partners – the rhetoric and the reality', *Harvard Business Review*, 69, 97–99.

Phizacklea, A. (1990) *Unpacking the Fashion Industry: Gender, Racism and Class in Production*, London: Routledge.

Prahalad, C.K. and Hamel, G. (1990) 'The core competences of the corporation', *Harvard Business Review*, 68, 79–91.

Tierney, M. and Williams, R. (1991) *Issues in the Black-boxing of Information Technologies*, Edinburgh University: PICT Working Paper, 22.

Webb, J. (1992) 'The mismanagement of innovation', *Sociology*, 26, 471–92.

Webb, J. and Dawson, P. (1991) 'Measure for measure: strategic change in an electronic instruments corporation', *Journal of Management Studies*, 28, 191–206.

Weber, M. (1948) 'On bureaucracy', in H.H. Gerth and C. Wright-Mills (eds) *Max Weber: Essays in Sociology*, London: Routledge.

Williamson, O.E. (1975) *Markets and Hierarchies: Analysis and Antitrust Implications*, New York: Free Press.

Williamson, O.E. (1986) *Economic Organisation: Firms, Markets and Policy Control*, Brighton: Wheatsheaf.

Wood, S. (1989) 'New wave management?', *Work, Employment and Society*, 3, 379–402.

Zuboff, S. (1988) *In the Age of the Smart Machine*, New York: Heinemann.

Index